garden

AUSTRALIAN
HOUSE
&GARDEN

garden

ACPbooks

the
new
garden

Today, many of us work indoors. Perhaps that's why we long to be outdoors whenever we can. Luckily, we live in the perfect place for that to happen – Australia, the land of opportunity, where dreams become reality and a patch of land is there to own. When the first settlers arrived, the earth yielded fruit and vegetables to nurture a new nation. Nowadays, our sophisticated supermarkets do that very nicely and so our garden nurtures us in innumerable other ways. For some it's a place to plant with a profusion of colour and texture, for others the garden is home to a pool in which family and friends can frolic. Then again, as our lifestyle makes eating a more casual occasion, the garden has fast become the centre of attention for all sorts of entertaining. And, as the open architectural approach to our homes makes the outdoor vista so important, so the design of our gardens has taken on renewed importance.

contents

This Brisbane garden is reminiscent of ancient temple ruins set amid lush tropical plantings. The owners wanted a peaceful space where they could display their Asian sculptures and urns.

today's gardens

The Australian 'backyard' has grown up. No longer defined by a stretch of lawn and a Hills Hoist, it has evolved into a multi-faceted organism, as individual as its owners. Today's gardens are more than just leafy patches of green, bright splashes of colour, or grounds for growing championship roses. The garden does duty as an extra room; one perfect for entertaining, nurturing, or simply being. It is a cocoon, a haven, a retreat. In fact, if the kitchen is the heart of a home, the garden represents its soul. Within each garden are any number of usable spaces, designed to embrace and to be embraced. Here, we look at 12 such spaces. You probably call one or all of them the essence of the soul of your home.

1. TRANSITION SPACE

Where once the house and garden were separate entities, with boundaries clearly marked at the back door, now the relationship is more complicated. Houses are being opened up for light and space, often resulting in transparent walls of glass providing the only barrier between them and the garden. Bi-fold doors are creating new ideas for indoor and outdoor living, and many homes are being extended under pergolas or covered paved areas just beyond the back door. Blurring the lines even further, the focus of our homes has changed. Whereas in Victorian times we presented our best front to the world in formal parlours and formal gardens, now we are likely to save our best for the back, inviting guests to share informal meals in our glass-and-space edifices. This transition area provides a key for casual and comfortable modern living, and calls for gardens that make the grade. Why open up the view, after all, if the view is not up to it? *There's a Zen simplicity to this Sydney inner-city semi-detached house. The owner/architect is a great fan of Japanese and modernist design and she's cleverly connected the indoors with the outdoors by using hard landscaping and plants in a grid-like design echoing the Shoji-style sliding glass walls. Steps in the courtyard double as seats for when there's a crowd.*

2. WATER FEATURE

It's hard to imagine now that there was ever a time in which every Australian garden did *not* have a water feature, or one in the planning. Water has been incorporated into modern garden design as prolifically as it once was in the gardens of ancient civilisations, such as Egypt and Persia, creating havens in dusty, dry landscapes. Today, water trickles and splashes from fountains and wall plaques, or lies still in deep, reflective pools, encouraging contemplation. In our increasingly dry landscape, it provides a cooling element. *The indoor and outdoor spaces of this Adelaide home formally merge, with surprises at every turn, such as the elegant fish pond cut into the terrace paving and fed by a trickling fountain. The owners love the fact that they can view the pond through the dining room's seamless glass walls and listen to the relaxing sounds of the water from the adjoining sunken conversation area.*

3. WALLED GARDEN

The idea of a cool space within a built environment is not a new one. Courtyards, whether internal or external, have been included in construction since the times of the ancient Romans and Greeks. Today's cities are so closely assembled and so heavily populated, however, that the importance of that small space is magnified. As likely to act as an extension of the house as a garden per se, today's courtyards can be furnished and painted, dug up and planted, or simply concreted or paved. Making the most of the small space available is the key, achieved by the use of vertical screenings, climbing flowering plants, water features as wide as your hand, and ledges and walls for perching upon. The personality that can be imprinted on these box-like enclosures is limited only by the imagination. *The artist owner of this house in Melbourne has capitalised on the intimate scale and high walls of her courtyard to turn it into a private outdoor room. She moved her furnishings and artworks outside to create the perfect setting in which to relax. Painted walls tone in with the textured 'floor' of flagstones and small flat pebbles set in concrete. Her own sculpture is highlighted against an abstract painting.*

2

3

4

5

6

4. AROUND THE CLOCK

We're maximising places and potential for living. No apartment nowadays, for instance, is complete without a balcony for contemplation and entertaining. But it's not just space in our lives that we're maximising – we're making the most of time as well. Gardens at night used to be quiet places, full of shadows and secret rustlings. Sophisticated lighting techniques are, however, extending their use around the clock. The garden that is merely beautiful during the day takes on a magical aura at night. *Perched on the corner of a converted office building in Melbourne's inner city, this tiny balcony was exposed and windy. But, with clever planting and lighting by a landscape designer, the space was remodelled into a stylish night and day entertaining space. Hardy, wind-resistant privet hedges, conical myrtle and English box topiaries help create a sense of enclosure. Nothing is permanent, making it an ideal solution for those who rent.*

5. GARDEN ROOMS

As upfront as our national character, Australian gardens used to be put together with a 'what-you-see-is-all-you-see' approach. Today's suburban backyard, however, is likely to incorporate a series of garden 'rooms', even if it's merely a pergola here, a screened utility area there, and a children's play area under a tree. Taking a leaf from a garden design philosophy practised by English novelist and poet Vita Sackville-West (famous for her garden at Sissinghurst Castle in Kent) and French landscape designer André La Nôtre (responsible for the gardens at Versailles), Australians are creating gardens full of surprises, revealed only as visitors move through them. *This mountain garden has large curved garden beds planted with huge rhododendrons that act as a focal point of colour while obscuring what's around the corner. A glimpse of a pergola draws you, both visually and physically, into another garden 'room'.*

6. PRODUCTIVITY

It is a reflection on our history of immigration that Australian menus contain so many diverse ingredients. One way to bring memories with us from our homelands is to grow them. Modern gardeners grow their own fruit, vegetables and herbs as a way to reach out to their heritage, and to keep in touch with the seasons and cycles of the earth. An increased interest in the origins of food also sees more people putting cabbages in with their cabbage roses. *This walled garden is reminiscent of the formal kitchen gardens used for centuries at large English manor houses to feed entire households. Designed around a central bed with a paved path running around each plot for easy access, the garden is both productive and conducive to relaxation as both owners enjoy gardening. A small buxus hedge contains each plot, dividing up types of vegetables and creating a neat uniform look that also suits the formal house style.*

7

8

7. THE SIDE GARDEN

In keeping with the idea of a home that's encircled by greenery comes the development of the smaller parts of your garden. The front garden has always played an important role for the house proud. It is here that we project an image to our street. It is here that we express our individuality or, in some cases, our sense of belonging. Today, however, the side garden also has a role. As our fences grow along with our defences, particularly in cities, the side garden may be the only link we have with our neighbours. We use it constantly for movement from the face we show to the world (the front garden) to the heart of our personal life (the back garden), and it takes on a little of the personality of each.

A subdivision has left this house with little more than this side garden which culminates in an entertaining area. Bathroom tiles were smashed into mosaics and laid with slate to create the path; black mondo grass infills. A slatted fence in the same blue adds winter colour when the maples shed their leaves.

8. ROOMS WITH VIEWS

Australian gardens are taking on a more nurturing role, encircling houses to provide a soothing view from every room. Light and airy bathrooms are positioned to allow an uplifting vista in the morning. Bedrooms, becoming less about sleeping and more about personal sanctuaries, are adorned with window boxes full of night-fragrant plants. Trees are underplanted with colour and greenery; statuary is used to provide a focal point. Every aspect of the house is treated to an axis point in the garden, allowing us to feel surrounded by nature at her best.

This new house has been designed around a central courtyard. All living rooms and the main bedroom open onto the four-metre-square patio, which is flagged with sandstone pavers and decorated with reconstituted stone planter pots. Feature tiles pick up the blue hue of the paintwork and are subtly outlined with pebble edging.

9. FAMILY MATTERS

The backyard has traditionally been a child's domain and, while adults are increasingly finding a haven in the garden, it remains the focus of a child's world. Even a small space holds unlimited possibilities for young imaginations. Modern garden design allows playground equipment to be integrated with sophisticated entertaining spaces. Plantings can be chosen to be hard-wearing and beautiful. Design your garden to provide not only a place for children to play, but a place in which they can learn, explore and discover the natural world.

The owner of this garden is an occupational therapist and wanted it to be both a visual and a sensory treat for children with coordination and learning difficulties, including autism. As these children love patterns, she created swirly pathways, mazes and chequerboard designs. For tactile play, the garden features trailing natives, mulch floors, herbs, grasses and pavers.

12

climbing rose, 'Lamarque', and the crimson rambler, 'Bloomfield Courage', are used for the colourful arch. Yellow spears of Wachendorfia *pick up the* Kniphofia *'Candlelight' and yellow mustard called 'Big Red'. Another yellow favourite is* Verbascum olympicum, *the large-leafed plant just about to burst into flower.*

12. THE ENTERTAINERS

When this elusive 'lifestyle' is portrayed in advertising, selling us an ideal world, it often involves people, food and the great outdoors. We are simply in love with the combination of entertaining and alfresco, and garden design reflects this passion. Paved areas, outdoor furniture, perhaps even a sleek barbecue, are all elements of the modern garden. The 'entertaining area' is a vital new dimension for garden designers to incorporate, and one that most people demand. After all, it seems criminal to create a beautiful space and then not be able to use it fully!

A small courtyard, once a sad stretch of poor neglected grass that wouldn't grow, has been paved and coloured to create a divine dining space. A water feature cascades down vivid blue steps, a creeping fig climbs up pink rendered walls – the result is dynamic enough to be a conversation piece when friends come to feast. White paving and dining equipment do nothing to detract from the drama of the scene.

10. PERSONAL SPACE

Psychologists agree that each of us needs a space to call our own. Without a small corner of the earth that's ours alone, we have nowhere to hide, nowhere to regroup, nowhere to metaphorically count to 10. The garden is often the place to which we turn for that moment of respite. So our gardens are taking on more personality. Courtyards today are as likely to contain an effigy of a Hindu goddess as a small pot-plant collection. Balconies will be painted in vibrant colours and peopled with garden gnomes, if that's what the gardener fancies. Green spaces will feature original sculptures and works of art, as we take our aesthetic ideals beyond the house walls. We draw energy from our gardens when

needed; we also let them draw away our stress. And there's no better place to sunbake.
Perches and plinths in this Brisbane garden allow the owners to display their collection of Asian sculptures and urns. Although it looks well established, this garden is only a couple of years old. The owners wanted a peaceful space and the designer has answered the brief by creating a 'temple garden' that seems relocated from some exotic Asian location.

11. HOBBY GARDEN

We speak of the fast-moving pace of society today and yet, in many ways, we move more slowly and less than ever before. Gardening allows us to exercise at a gentle pace. It also lets us enjoy an interactive

relationship with the world. We do more than passively watch a garden, as we do a television screen. We touch, we cherish, we dig, we water, we feed, in some cases we destroy, in others we raise again. The art of gardening is enjoying ever-increasing popularity among the young and a new-found respect among older people. Today, however, we nurture more than just plants. Through gardening, we cultivate 'lifestyle', that elusive and seductive modern ideal.
The owner of this garden is a 'plantsman': he buys whatever he likes and just sticks it in. He happily overplants, he allows his garden to escape beyond his front picket fence, and he has a penchant for blowsy varieties such as delphiniums and for the bold colour of red. The white

front gardens

welcome

The Great Australian Dream has been traditionally represented by the quarter-acre block, conjuring up images of stretches of bucolic backyard, but it's the verdant patch between house and street that immediately invokes the personality of the dreamer. The front garden has always provided a canvas on which to present our best 'faces' to society. It's here that initial impressions are created; here that the transition from outside world to inner sanctum begins. To understand the implications of that short journey from gate to front door, it's important to consider the long and sometimes difficult voyage of Australian gardeners from our earliest European settlements to the present day.

the great australian dream

In his official report in 1788, Governor Arthur Phillip proposed "that when houses are to be built here, the grants of land shall be made with such clauses as will prevent the building of more than one house on one allotment, which is to consist of sixty feet in front, and one hundred and fifty feet in depth. These regulations will preserve a kind of uniformity in the buildings, prevent narrow streets, and exclude many inconveniences which a rapid increase of inhabitants might otherwise occasion hereafter". These dimensions have remained fairly constant until recent times.

In the 18th century, overcrowding was seen as the root cause of crime in England and something to be avoided. Housing was one of Phillip's priorities. Another was feeding a population without the skills needed to produce its own food. The two were seen as co-dependent. The quarter-acre block not only allowed for uncramped living but also provided enough land for people to grow food – vegetables, fruit and poultry. The backyard vegetable patch was born.

LANDSCAPE ROOTS

Australia was settled at the precise moment that the English landscape school was in its prime. Its influence extended to the estates of colonial merchants who established landscape parks. >

CALIFORNIA BUNGALOW

This inter-war architectural style originated on the American west coast. However, by the early 1920s, Australian architects and speculative builders had already embraced the California bungalow style with their own interpretation. Built in brick rather than timber and featuring rough-cast exterior walls, a low-pitched tiled roof and shingled gables, the houses were deemed suitable for Australia's sunny climate. Gardens tended to have areas of lawn, with imported plants used in preference to natives. This house (left) has been renovated, with the exterior painted to modernise its appearance. The owners have embraced a more formal concept for their front garden, layering the colour, pattern and texture of the plants to frame the house.

1950s HOUSE

The suburban post-war house was built on a large block (many on the traditional quarter-acre), but the front garden was fairly small. There were straight concrete pathways bisecting neat flower beds and specimen trees. The lawn was mowed religiously and used often for children's ball games. In today's renovating climate, both houses and gardens have great potential for updating. You can use shrubs to shelter windows like these owners have (opposite), or plant a shady tree, such as this impressive weeping fig, to act as a barrier to the street. Rather than have distinct rows of colourful annuals, the owners have mass-planted a central bed with a blazing display of pansies, anemones and ranunculus, with white alyssum highlights.

< Adaptation was essential: Norfolk Island pines and other araucarias replaced the pines and cedars of English designs in early gardens such as Old Government House and Elizabeth Farm, both in Parramatta, and Vaucluse House in Sydney.

The ideal of a house with land and garden was thus established as worthy of emulation by other classes. Most of the population, however, lived in small houses and practised some form of urban agriculture for survival. Orchards, kitchen gardens and herbs were planted with a few flowers around rough wattle-and-daub houses, setting a pattern seen in Australian homes for nearly two centuries. In part, the self-sufficiency ethic

has driven the 'Great Australian Dream' of the quarter-acre block. It provided land for living and space for all.

In British cities, suburbs were spreading outside the crowded heart. As early as 1810, in bustling industrial Birmingham, Lord Calthorpe established Edgbaston, an estate that predated the later 'garden city' concept by decades. Soon after, John Claudius Loudon, an English garden writer, popularised new types of gardens that reacted to the change in block size and expanding suburban development. Loudon's writings were geared not to the gentry but to the emerging middle class and, as such, were avidly consumed in the new colony of Australia.

>

TROPICAL HOUSE

Elevated houses are typical in Darwin and the coastal tropical regions of Australia, where climate is the prime consideration. Originally, in the early 1900s, the houses would have been built of timber and raised on wooden stumps, but today many elevated houses are planned as separate sections linked by open passages and built in lightweight timber, steel and corrugated iron. Elevating a house allows cooling air movement while creating a space that is high enough for under-house storage and children's play. In some situations, it is where the family keeps the laundry. So as not to restrict air flow, this lower level is only partially enclosed by lattice or sturdier timber battens. Privacy is maintained around this contemporary Darwin home (opposite) with cycads, tropical shrubs and narrow trees planted to give visual interest at different heights. The close planting of native gums offers a leafy outlook from the upper storey windows while a cordyline and a potted ficus help screen the utility area under the house. While it's good to create a 'screen' made up of an interesting variety of plants, the fact that they must be able to withstand distinct wet and dry seasons does limit plant choice.

FEDERATION HOME

During the later years of Australia's Federation period, there was a strong push to create model garden suburbs. The idea came from half a world away in Great Britain, where the revolutionary 'new thinking' of city planners was to give people more living space, expanding cities from a hub of sub-standard tenements into the surrounding green acres. Australia, eager to follow the Mother Country's lead, quickly passed new planning laws. Houses built in the early 1920s in these garden suburbs were single-family bungalows with sufficient space for a garden. A well-kept garden was a heavily symbolic element, mirroring the 'community-mindedness' of the owner. The idea was to have flowers, grass, shrubs and trees merging as a whole, and many of the gardens consequently required considerable maintenance. Federation houses are traditionally dark brick but, where owners find the bricks too heavy, the walls can be screened by verdant creepers and vines. The owners of this Federation cottage (above) are passionate gardeners and around the entrance and windows they've planted pretty, redolent star jasmine, hellebores, clipped box hedges and roses which highlight the architectural detailing.

NEOCLASSICAL

*The façade of this recently built family home (left) takes its inspiration from the houses of the Mediterranean, mixing practicality with elegance and featuring a roof of Spanish tiles, softly arched windows and a portico supported by a pair of cast concrete columns. Unpolished Indian limestone borders a slate pathway, while English box hedging encloses white 'Iceberg' standard roses, white petunias and tall, slender, dark green pencil pines (*Cupressus sempervirens*).*

ARCHITECT DESIGNED

Contemporary architecture can impose limitations on the style of a front garden. The architecture of this house (opposite top), however, set no boundaries. Inspired by the water feature near the entrance to the house, the landscaper decided to expand on the theme outdoors to present the house as 'under water'. She designed a river-shaped bed of smooth pebbles set into a lawn of 'Greenlees Park' couch grass and planted with seaweed-like mother-in-law's tongues. The coral-like branches of a frangipani tree offer a surreal image against the boldly coloured walls.

PROVINCIAL FUSION

This style (opposite bottom) combines classic Australian country architecture with a French-provincial garden. Inspiration comes from the rustic cottages of the south of France and Tuscany with their grapevine-covered arbours and lavender hedges. Elements of an Italian Renaissance garden, such as symmetry and discipline, are used here, too. While regular pruning is required for the box and gardenia hedges, a restricted number of plants makes maintenance simple. Here, jacaranda and clumps of agapanthus key in the garden's signature colour, blue.

< One of Loudon's dissertations was 'The Suburban Gardener and Villa Companion of 1838'. In it he wrote, "A suburban residence, with a small portion of land attached, will contain all that is essential for happiness." To him, the suburb escaped city clamour, substituting a quasi-rural existence "where man may approach the simplicity of nature and attain the enjoyments and pleasures of pristine innocence". In Australia, such sentiments reinforced the long-held dream of the quarter-acre block.

RISE OF THE SUBURBS

Governor Darling established the first Australian suburbs near Woolloomooloo, granting allotments to wealthy merchants in the early 1830s. These first suburbs were socially mixed. In the days before mechanised transport, the city was a pedestrian zone where transport was limited to horse-drawn wagons and coaches.

The 1840s and 1850s saw a period of rapid population growth. This was the result of mass immigration caused by the Irish famine, followed by the accumulation of rural wealth and the gold rush. To house all these new arrivals, terrace houses burgeoned but, without proper sewerage and sanitation, they soon became squalid. Tightly fitting terraces with no room for gardens had little more than a cesspit or outdoor toilet and a woodpile for fuel and cooking. There was no garden or anything resembling the trendy modern inner-city courtyard.

Developers cashed in with new suburbs on the city outskirts where people could escape these slums. New forms of >

VICTORIAN FACADE

This beautifully proportioned house (opposite) reflects a time of aggressive prosperity and pride. The two-storey verandah gained popularity as the Victorian period progressed. From the mid-19th century, a growing demand for more ornate styles of architecture led to the extensive use of decorative cast iron, which can be seen detailing this house. This filigree screen was the most visually dominant feature and gave the architecture its signature. Many freestanding houses were surrounded by a leafy garden. This front garden reveals a row of standard roses and flowering shrubs, along with formal hedges and garden beds for flowering annuals. An iron fence would have been common in a city house, however the owners of this one have installed a painted picket fence to tone down the formality of the exterior. When it comes to selecting the colours of plants, you can choose a contemporary palette, but opting for all-white flowers is a great idea as they look stunning in contrast to the dark-coloured fence.

MODERN ZEN APPROACH

Water is an important feature of the Japanese garden, providing atmosphere and encouraging contemplation and meditation. At the front of this suburban house (right), water has been introduced in the form of a shallow reflection pool, adding a new dimension with movement, sound and fluidity. You can design a pool to replace grass as a ground cover, and blend it with natural materials such as stone and granite. But remember that, as a design element, the pool should be integrated with the house and maintained like a swimming pool to ensure consistently clear blue water.

< transportation hastened this pattern. In Sydney, horse-drawn trams were introduced in 1861. Steam trams followed in Sydney in 1879 and in Melbourne in 1885, and new suburbs soon sprang up along the tramlines. With them came aspirations of a better life.

GARDEN CITY MOVEMENT

The twin scourges of poor sanitation and overcrowding led to a new breed of philanthropic industrialist in the United Kingdom. Robert Owen led the way in 1817 with a model village at New Lanark in Scotland. In the 1870s, a Garden City Movement lobbied for better forms of housing. In response, factory owners like George Cadbury, Joseph Rowntree and William Lever built suburbs that were clean and open, with space for

gardens and fruit trees – and contented employees. This international movement reached its peak between 1896 and 1916. In Australia, Haberfield and Daceyville in Sydney, the Colonel Light Gardens in Adelaide and Garden Suburb in Newcastle were designed and constructed according to the principles of the International Garden Cities Association. They were largely responsible for shaping the typical Australian suburb of today.

Daceyville was designed for returned soldiers to live in a 'home fit for heroes' – others were more speculative. As building of new subdivisions gathered pace, the quality was subtly degraded until the Depression dealt a killer blow. The main features survived, however, and our greatest example of all, Canberra, remained pure to the classic Garden City precepts.

If the backyard links Australians to our traditional 'wide open spaces', the front garden allows expression of our multicultural 'faces'. As the entrance point to the house, it creates the important first impression. Once, when the backyard was a purely functional space, the front garden was the real focus of aesthetic gardening. Newer housing styles and new directions in gardening, however, have transformed the front garden into a showpiece as well as a thoroughfare. Whether its style is compact and formal, large and sweeping, or a barely controlled ramble of colour, the front garden should combine creative inspiration with a practical approach.

planning a front garden

The main function of the front garden is to provide access. A wide, comfortable path leading to the front door will provide a welcoming entrance for family and visitors (for more on pathways, see page 33). Keep the access safe by clearing any obstructions: how welcome will visitors feel if they have to dodge overhanging branches on a wet day? Avoid plantings that need constant cutting back and remove slippery moss. Ensure that the house number is displayed prominently either on the house, at the front gate, or on the letterbox.

While the front garden is also the entry point for cars and parking, the driveway should not dominate the area. Disguise it through careful planting, positioning it to one side and using muted colours.

Because most of the family's outdoor activity now takes place behind the house, low-maintenance planting can be used at the front. Choose plants that provide privacy and that disguise off-street parking. For screening, use shrubs, repeating them, as in a hedge, or mixed with similar or contrasting shapes for maximum impact (and minimum outlay). For security, avoid screening the front door behind a mass of high shrubs that might offer intruders a hiding place.

LAYOUT AND DESIGN

House design changes with each decade and certain features are indicative of specific periods of architecture. So it is with plants and the way they are treated in a garden. In general, the planting, design and materials should be roughly consistent with the style of the house.

Design comes unstuck where an unsympathetic style is imposed on distinctive architecture. A formal, classical landscape design imposed on an ultra-modern steel-and-glass home, or perhaps a Santa Fe-desert look on an authentic Victorian façade, for instance, can look anachronistic and out of place. Some period architecture almost demands a garden design contemporary with its era and consistent with its architectural integrity. There are exceptions, of course, and a modern twist can be given to a period Victorian garden. New materials and cutting-edge design will always match if carried off with skill and panache.   >

A pathway of recycled brick leads from the front gate of this garden, through an encroaching jungle of cordyline, philodendron and mondo grass. Petunias and peace lilies beside the path provide colour.

< Similarly, certain design characteristics lend themselves to particular styles of garden. If the front door is set dead centre of a symmetrical façade, a garden with a straight central path and a formal design may be appropriate. An L-shaped façade demands an informal garden design with perhaps a winding path to the front door. Within these basic frameworks, it is possible to use either formal or informal garden elements to lend depth to the design. Hedges can give an informal garden structural strength, while perennials that are planted loosely behind low hedges will soften the harder lines of a formal garden.

LANDSCAPING MATERIALS

Choose the best materials for your budget. Stone is the most expensive paving and edging material but new forms of concrete made to resemble sandstone or limestone can be a good alternative and marginally cheaper. Local materials (those naturally occurring where you live) give a better match with the location and are generally less expensive than stone or products imported from interstate or overseas. They make it easier to achieve a 'sense of place' that distinguishes any garden.

BOUNDARY FENCES

Timber is the most popular fencing material in suburban yards. Fences form a solid boundary on three sides in the backyard but front yards are generally less enclosed. At the front, fences are often open in design and usually half the height of those in the back. This allows more scope for hedging, shrub screens and softer forms of decorative boundary.

If space is limited, for instance along a driveway, climbers can be grown on a wire fence to give a green border between your property and your neighbour's. A solid wall can create wind turbulence, which in turn can damage sensitive plants. Lattice fences and screens, however, can filter winds and provide partial privacy but still allow for light and views. (See *Entrances and Fences*, opposite.)

PLANTING PRINCIPLES

The rules for planting are simple, and apply not just to the front garden, but to every part. Grow plants suited to the conditions – climate, soil and frost. Choosing unsuitable plants creates extra work.

If you live in a humid coastal climate, avoid Mediterranean plants unless you have a dry microclimate with good air circulation. Similarly, avoid rainforest plants in dry inland zones.

Improve your soil before planting by adding manure, organic material, humus and soil conditioners. Once the plants are in the ground, water them well for the first 12 months to ensure the roots take a firm hold. This even applies to native plants and any that are grown for their drought tolerance – they need a season >

WHICH STYLE OF GARDEN SUITS YOUR HOME?

Victorian houses were often elaborately decorated with symmetrical façades and gardens that were ordered along geometric lines with parterres and well-clipped hedges. Symmetrical plantings vied with unusual, exotic plants as status symbols.

Workers' cottages (left) were built for the working class around 1900. They renovate well and many today feature attractive cottage gardens.

Federation houses were asymmetrical with a naturalistic style of garden. Plants were kept to the perimeter, with feature beds to set off an impressive lawn.

California bungalows featured a hedge-and-wire fence on the front boundary. Flowers were popular, particularly gladioli and roses.

Wartime and post-war houses of the 1940s and 1950s often featured a row of hybrid tea or a low, informal hedge of floribunda roses along the grass verge.

The 1970s was the era of the natives, touted as low-maintenance plants to match with a mood that saw gardens as work. Mini-forests of untamed bottlebrushes, grevilleas and short-lived wattles sprang up in front gardens.

The 1980s and 1990s were dominated by two contrasting garden styles. One was the cottage garden with mixed flowers randomly placed and the other was elaborate parterres, all-white gardens, low box hedging and romantic garden art.

The Noughties have seen architectural looks take a firm hold while outdoor living has become of paramount concern to owners as garden size shrinks.

ENTRANCES AND FENCES

The front door is a place for greetings and farewells. Overhead cover is vital for protection against the weather (**1**). Continue the visual theme by linking the style of entranceway with the boundary fence (**2**). Make the area in front of the door generous enough for two people to stand abreast (**3**). A pot of flowering annuals or an architectural plant that suits the style of the garden sets a welcoming tone (**4**). Before erecting any type of fence you must check with your council that the intended location will be correctly positioned on your property's boundary. Find out whether there are any local restrictions on design, size or height. If it's a side fence you're erecting or replacing, it's a matter of agreement with your neighbours. The cost of a necessary new fence between two properties is usually shared equally. For best effect, the style of fence should take inspiration from the architecture of your home. Composite fencing, when two or more materials – such as concrete and timber palings – are used together, is popular for contemporary house designs (**5**). Timber paling fences and painted picket fences are evergreen styles for houses with history, while durable Colorbond is practical in areas where heat, humidity and salt spray are factors. Thick hedges or high brick walls softened with climbing plants are functional for houses on busy roads where noise is an issue, or in closely populated inner-city suburbs to provide a measure of privacy.

< to establish. Later, reduce the artificial watering to toughen them to your conditions. They should then survive on natural rainfall except in the driest of times.

Always mulch after planting to conserve moisture, remembering to check underneath the mulch during summer to see if the ground is wet. Lift the mulch and scratch the top few centimetres of soil to see how much moisture has been retained. If it is dry, soak the area – a hose dribbling gently for an hour or so will saturate the ground more thoroughly than any sprinkler, which merely sprays water into the air, not down to the roots.

COLOUR

Colour in a garden comes from two major sources: the plants within it, and the hard surfaces, furniture, statuary and other ornamentation with which you choose to decorate it. When deciding upon a colour scheme for your garden, particularly your front garden, it's important to take into consideration the permanent colour with which you are dealing, whether it be the red brick of a Federation house, the blue stone of an Adelaide cottage, or the yellow-toned render of a Tuscan-style property. Of course, walls and fences can always be painted but, in most cases, particularly when it comes to the architectural features, it's most effective to work with what's there. There are so many colours in the plant world that it's easy to end up with a messy jumble, unless you plan carefully. How much colour you bring into your garden is up to you. Some might choose an all-white scheme, while others will love the contrast between bright oranges and pinks (which look great against a white, beige or cream house). To produce a harmonious scheme, you might choose to concentrate on either warm colours (reds, yellows, oranges) or cool colours (white, lemon, green and blue). If your house colours are very strong (such as red), a cool or restricted colour scheme will provide balance. Remember, too, that as seasons change, so do gardens, so it's important to plan for the changes that your selected plants will undergo throughout the year. No matter which colour scheme you might lean towards, however, the best place to start is with a colour wheel. This is essentially a circle divided into all the colours of the rainbow. It allows you to see at a glance the relationship between the different colours, the contrasts and the harmonies. You may choose, for example, to work with different tones of one colour (different degrees of brightness or strength) to create a garden of great harmony. Think of the reds – from the lightest pinks through to deepest crimson. Remember too that green in all its many variations will provide the backdrop for your plants. The different tones within a garden's foliage can create great textural interest for those floral lean times. And a green-on-green garden offers the ultimate in contemporary looks.

MAINTENANCE

Because the front garden is mostly a showpiece, we tend to spend less time there. Plantings need to be designed for low maintenance and long-term effect. Hedges present a clean, crisp edge to the front boundary in keeping with the more formalised style of entrance, while borders of flowering shrubs and groundcovers add the vitality of colour through the seasons. The contemporary trend is for less emphasis on seasonal plants. To keep the garden looking good all year, bulbs and annuals can be planted in large pots to be removed and replanted when their flowering finishes. Mulching and irrigation systems save water by reducing evaporation, plus saving time and effort by reducing weeds and hand watering.

LIGHTING

Lighting in the front garden is all about show and safety. It can create a mood by highlighting features such as a well-shaped tree, a fountain or a special pot. Primarily, however, it should enhance access to your front door at night, and improve security by removing the shadows that can cloak the work of prowlers. (For more on lighting, see page 61.)

PATHWAYS

In the front garden, all pathways lead to the front door. How they get there, however, is up to you. While many people opt for the simple, direct line from gate to door, others may choose to make the journey a little more interesting. You can add a curve, for instance, as long as there's a reason for it (garden bed, water feature), or broaden your path and add a feature tree or statue as a focal point. You can even hide your front door through clever use of planting and garden design, and have your path meander up to it via a scenic route. Whatever design you decide upon, a path needs to be tough enough to take lots of wear-and-tear and, importantly, needs to be non-slip. Your pathways can also add textural interest to your garden, beyond that provided by foliage and flowers. There are a number of options in hard surfacing suitable for pathways: mix them up for an individual touch.

Brick/pavers: a weathered look can be achieved by using recycled bricks laid in sand or concrete. Various patterns, from herringbone to basketweave, can be used in paving (**1**), or gaps left between bricks for planting, perhaps, chamomile. Ensure that you do not allow moss to build up on the bricks, as this will become slippery.

Stone: large slabs of stone or stone pavers offer a natural effect, though in contemporary patterns they add a touch of elegance to a garden. Stepping stones (**2**), on the other hand, offer a fey quality, and are suited to non-functional paths (such as leading to a water feature). Natural stone, such as granite, limestone, sandstone and slate, occurs in many different colours.

Concrete: where it was once a dull choice for a pathway, concrete has come into its own in recent years, with the introduction of coloured and textured varieties.

Tiles: need to be chosen with non-slip properties in mind. They are best suited to short paths and front steps, and can be laid in simple patterns or complex mosaics.

Gravel: needs an edging of brick, wood or concrete to contain it within the parameters of your path. It varies in colour from white to black or brown, and shades between.

Pebbles: come in many sizes and can be loose or set in concrete in patterns (**3**).

Timber/decking: works well if the site slopes or is uneven, as it can be constructed to provide a smooth transition between levels. It's particularly effective in rural settings and near water (**4**).

COTTAGE GARDENS

1. Japanese windflowers (*Anemone x hybrida*) are perennials with white or pink flowers for a partially shaded garden but tolerating full sun if given moist, rich, well-drained soil. Climate: cool-subtropical.

2. Foxgloves (*Digitalis purpurea*) give height to this colourful mixed border. The tall flower spires of these dramatic biennials open progressively up the stem. They flower in spring in sun to light shade and love a moist, rich, well-drained soil. Climate: cool-subtropical.

3. Salvias, with their spires of red and blue flowers, and asters gently spill over and into the path. Climate: cool-subtropical.

4. Roses are hard to beat in a sunny front garden. They come in all shapes and sizes, from ground covers to standards and climbers; planted year round. Climate: suitable for all types (but best in cool to temperate).

5. Italian lavender (*Lavandula stoechas*) and other lavender varieties can be planted year round in full sun and a well-drained soil. Include a handful of lime at planting. Prune after flowering. Climate: cool-temperate (Mediterranean best).

ANNUALS

Annuals, also known as seedlings or bedding plants, are grown from seed or bought already growing in punnets or small pots. Use the colours of annuals to enhance those of the house or of the boundary walls or fences. They can also act as a focal point to show the way to the front door. Annuals are planted a season ahead of when they are expected to flower and can be grown in the ground, in pots or in hanging baskets. Seasonal highlights to grow in your front garden include: pansy, poppy, polyanthus, primula and viola for spring; begonia, cleome, impatiens, petunia and phlox for summer; aster, Californian poppy, chrysanthemum, cosmos and dahlia for autumn;

calendula, cineraria, cyclamen, pansy and wallflower for winter. Keep all annuals at their best by applying an organic mulch around each plant and providing a liquid feed every two to three weeks. Remove spent flowers and give any that become leggy an all-over haircut with shears or secateurs. Within around six weeks, they should be full of new growth and flowering again. Long, lanky growth that can occur in fast-growing annuals, such as petunias, can be avoided by pinching out the growing tips when the plants are still young. And remember these plants are easy to remove and cheap to replace with fresh new seedlings, or even with small potted plants for instant colour.

6. Calendulas, which can flower all year round, are at their best in winter. Grow them from seedlings planted in late summer to autumn in a sunny, well-drained spot. Colours include vivid shades of yellow, orange and brown.

7. Violas are really just small pansies. Most are compact, long-flowering plants and some are delightfully fragrant. Keep them well watered, particularly as the cool days of winter give way to warmer spells in spring, and they'll keep flowering. Some will self-sow and regrow each year.

8. Cosmos is one of the easiest of all annuals to grow and can be started from seed or seedling. Dwarf white cosmos only reach 60cm tall but you

can also enjoy taller growing plants to 100cm. All like full sun and are great for picking. Colours include pink, mauve, yellow and white.

9. Pansies, for winter to spring flowers, are planted from autumn to late winter. They do best in a sunny spot but need partial shade in a warm climate. Look for seedlings or small pots for instant colour. Colours include blue, purple, yellow, orange, brown, pink and white, along with bicolours and mixes. Many have cute striped faces.

10. Iceland poppies are vibrant winter to spring flowering annuals that love a sunny patch sheltered from strong winds. As they burst into bloom, the hairy buds split open to let the silky petals unfurl.

SCULPTURAL

Clipping and shaping plants introduces a formal and well-organised element to a front garden. Plants can be trained as a living fence such as a hedge, or shaped into a border to edge a path or act as a focal point. To bring structure and form to a garden, select an evergreen hedge. Choose shrubs, small trees or even climbers to make your sculptural statement. Some great hedging and edging choices include green, flowering and coloured-leaf plants such as abelia, azalea, box, camellia, conifers, duranta, honeysuckle (*Lonicera nitida*), lillypilly, murraya, photinia and star jasmine. Remember that where plants are closely grouped in a small area such as a hedge, they face root competition and

need extra water and food to compensate. Where tall plants are selected for a small area, for example a tall cypress as a 3m hedge, clipping is an ongoing commitment. Invest in a pair of good-quality powered shears with an extension handle. Hedges need to be clipped regularly while they are growing. Expect to clip most hedges two or three times a year, from spring to early autumn. Fertilise and water well after pruning to encourage strong new growth. Where hedges need to be straight, don't rely on your eye alone; use a string line for a level look. Here are different styles of hedges to ornament, border or divide your front garden, along with some of the best hedging choices.

1. Azaleas, such as this pink-flowered 'Alphonse Andersen', make a neat clipped flowering hedge 1-2m tall. Azaleas flower in late winter to early spring, so wait until after flowering to begin clipping. Some varieties also flower in autumn. Azaleas tolerate sun to light shade and benefit from an organic mulch over their shallow roots. Fertilise in spring.

2. Japanese box (*Buxus microphylla* var. *japonica*) and a strip of black mondo grass provide hedging in contrasting colours. This would be a smart choice to edge the front path. Dwarf box (*B. sempervirens* var. *suffruticosa*) can be used instead of Japanese box.

3. A stepped hedge uses rows of plants of differing heights, such as tall murraya (2-3m) in

the background, with gardenia, box, dwarf lillypilly or other evergreen compact shrubs in layers in front. Here, star jasmine forms the front edge. Maintain the stepped look with regular clipping, deep watering once or twice a week, and fertiliser in spring and late summer.

4. Star jasmine is adaptable to sun or shade so is a great choice to unify different parts of the garden. It is a climber if encouraged upwards, or a ground cover if allowed to spread over the ground. This is a plant that can be trained and shaped as desired. Its white flowers are deliciously fragrant.

5. Murraya, with its dense evergreen growth, is a good choice for hedging. As an added benefit it has flushes of cream, orange-blossom-scented flowers from spring to autumn. Flowering is best in full sun and after heavy rain.

6. Photinia has long been a popular hedging plant. After

clipping it produces flushes of bright red new growth, as is seen here on 'Red Robin'.

7. Camellias are another excellent hedging choice with green shiny growth all year, particularly in shade or filtered sun. In autumn, winter and into spring, you can enjoy their white, pink or red flowers.

8. Carolina jasmine (*Gelsemium sempervirens*) is a winter to spring flowering climber that can be used to cover a wall, fence or lattice screen. Keep it trained and clipped after flowering to encourage compact growth.

9. Teucrium (*T. fruticans*), with its grey leaves, has been clipped into a low, narrow hedge. The colour of the hedge accentuates the bare trunks of the lemon-scented gums.

For many Australians the pool is a symbol of everything that's fabulous about this country – great weather, good mates, family fun and superb outdoor eating and entertaining – which is why it is so often the focus of the back garden, as it is here.

back gardens

Australians have discovered that the best place to 'go out' is just outside the back door. In search of sanctuary in an increasingly complex world, we create a private universe within our gardens where entertaining (and living) is easy. Made to measure and with every modern convenience, these pleasure zones have everything but complications. Designed to conjure up that desirable, intangible spirit known as 'lifestyle', today's gardens are more than a view from the kitchen — they're more likely to embrace the indoors, drawing it (and you) outside.

inventing the backyard

Up until the post-war period in the late 1940s and 1950s, the backyard in Australian cities was a purely functional space. City backyards and rural yards fulfilled much the same purpose. There was an outdoor toilet, a washhouse, clothesline and a shed or two, perhaps with a woodpile or a workbench. For the most part, the backyard was a sort of post-agrarian, urban farm devoted to a degree of self-sufficiency. At first, it was more a man's domain than a woman's. Here he grew vegetables, made items for the house and, later, tinkered with the car. There was a patch of lawn where the kids could play and maybe a few plants

on the perimeter, but the idea of a back garden with flowerbeds, a tennis court and a patio was mostly the preserve of the wealthier middle classes.

One hundred years ago, the modern notion of a disposable income was inconceivable, so gardening was strictly a do-it-yourself art. Cuttings were exchanged, seeds sown and plants propagated at home rather than bought from the nursery in flower or fully grown. Gardens were self-sufficient, a product of economic circumstances in the boom and bust and war-torn decades of the late 19th and early 20th century.

Employing a gardener or a landscape >

THE NEW PERGOLA
A pergola not only offers structural support for climbing plants and shade during the hot summer months, it also frames the garden beautifully by drawing the eye to distinctive features. This one (above) is a far cry from the mission-brown structures that studded the suburban backyards of the 1960s. It shadows a sandstone path planted with Armeria maritima *which bursts with pretty pink blooms in spring. A fast-growing crimson glory vine (Vitis coignetiae) provides shade for an area which the owners and their pets use on a regular basis.*

USING THE LAWN

It's lovely to feel grass between your toes. Not everyone will have vast areas of velvety soft lawn, but many of us can manage a patch to spread out on and use in ways other than as a depository for kids' toys and play equipment. Here, the owners of a small suburban cottage have designated a section of lawn for entertaining purposes (opposite). The area is protected from breezes by a high wall screened with camellias and euphorbia. They've set a picnic table in the garden with bergenias and hyacinth. The emphasis here is on enjoying the outdoor ambience to its fullest. Be prepared to move the table and benches regularly as, with shading and continual wear underfoot, any lawn will turn to mud after heavy rain.

PERFECT PAVING

The durability of your paving determines how it will be used. With a fully enclosed outdoor space on the same level as the living room (right), the paving should have a connection with what's happening inside. It will need to withstand constant traffic and the movement of furniture. The crazy-paving effect seen here has been created with marble offcuts in different colours. The design begins at the sliding glass doors in a pinky brown stone (to complement the brushbox flooring inside) and 'flows' like molten lava in a curve, changing colour as it goes. Paving should always be well-drained and this courtyard has a central drain to take the run-off from heavy downpours.

< designer was out of the reach of most people. Edna Walling designed gardens for middle-class clients in the 1920s and her designs were more structured than most at the time. They may have had a cottage-style front yard, while in the back garden the space was broken into linked compartments with, perhaps, a terrace, a pergola, stone paths and a lawn.

Australian nurseries stocked mostly exotic plants and most would have been familiar to English gardeners with some adjustment to our climatic differences. Gardens were traditional and used a limited range of plants. It was almost unknown to use native plants in the home garden other than a few local trees and the odd bottlebrush. Edna Walling started to employ them by mid-century, but it took a long time to catch on. By the

1970s, the backyard was becoming more of a back garden that offered an escape from cares. Now, at the beginning of the 21st century, it has become a resort.

WE'VE COME A LONG WAY

Change began in the 1950s. American sitcoms – *Dennis The Menace, My Three Sons, Leave It To Beaver* – showed us the value of the outdoor terrace, the barbecue and the basketball hoop in the backyard. This Californication of the Australian backyard rested on ideals of leisure, outdoor living and structured plantings.

Even so, the suggestion that an adult entertaining space with an outdoor kitchen be included in the layout of a garden was unheard of in the suburbs. The house was the house and the garden was where the kids were sent to play. >

OUTDOOR FURNITURE

We're often swayed by appearance when it comes to choosing furniture for outside. It can have more to do with the suggestion of a lifestyle than with the notion of comfort. This patio (left) takes the concept of an elegant formal dining room and brings it out into the open. The owner's choice of stone and metal furniture shows a respect for the formal architecture; gently diffused light through louvred roof and window shutters emphasises the linear look. A cycad in a tall urn and clipped hedges provide an understated elegance in the planting scheme. The composite stone refectory table blends with stone paving, while metal chairs provide strong contrast. Cushions have been added to make the seats more comfortable. It's paramount to consider the comfort factor when entertaining.

THE PARTY SPACE

Take the opportunity to transform your back garden into the perfect party venue. This paved courtyard (opposite) is a potted garden, where plants such as citrus, camellia and ivy are clipped and shaped. The weeping standard acts as a living umbrella. Privacy and noise is often an issue with neighbours, so be considerate in your preparations. You can bank tall potted trees for a windbreak and hang a canvas sail or canopy for privacy. You can also make a temporary screen with timber lattice. It's a good idea to have things portable: plants in pots and lightweight furniture on castors, market umbrellas, hurricane lamps to protect candles from the wind, and plenty of unbreakable tableware. And don't forget the fairy lights.

< The barbecue was rudimentary – a metal grate built into Besser blocks. The Hills Hoist washing line stood proud at the end of a central pathway dissecting the lawn. The only concession to an outdoor living space was an open verandah or sleep-out which had a striped canvas roller blind you could pull down to create privacy for an extra sleeping space.

It wasn't until the 1960s and 1970s, with the emphasis on reclaiming our native bush, that our backyards began to change focus. Swimming pools, cabanas and paved terraces were included along with the rockery and native garden. People shifted family entertaining from the lounge room to the outdoors and pool parties were all the rage. Kids still ruled the backyard and parents supervised them through the kitchen window.

During this time, architects built houses that were quite different from the post-war box-like bungalows. Many houses were split-level with timber decks and balconies. Any landscaping made use of informally planted Australian natives. The timber pergola, usually painted in mission brown, became a useful structure for extending the ground-floor area of a house and thus supplied that first architectural link with the outdoors. The area was paved with bricks or slate, and it was a serious attempt at creating a formalised outdoor entertaining space.

LINKING INDOORS AND OUT

The old British tradition of life lived at the front of the house near the street has finally been banished. The standard approach to renovation these days is the >

ON THE VERANDAH

With its colonial origins, the verandah is important in Australian architecture because it particularly addresses our climate. Over the centuries, it has never lost its popularity. However, as a transition space, it has more to do with looking out and adjusting to the light patterns, than actually relaxing. The idea of the verandah has carried over to contemporary architecture where it translates as a deck with a roof. In this contemporary beach house in South Australia (opposite), the wrap-around verandah is shielded from extreme summer sun by angled awnings that still allow in light during the winter. The owners have made it a place to entertain, sit down with a cool drink, or sunbake. Sliding glass doors open wide onto the verandah from two sides, ushering in sea breezes that provide cross-ventilation.

INDOOR TO OUTDOOR

Acknowledging our temperate weather, we have embraced the concept of indoor/outdoor living. The designer/owner of this small Sydney house (right) blurred the boundaries by opening up his living room to a tiny courtyard, using colour and shape to emphasise the transition zone. Concertina doors save space, while decking extends the living room's polished boards. Greenery pokes through a timber fence, softening its look.

< exploitation of light and space, where the interior is opened up with vaulted ceilings, glazed walls and concertina doors in recognition of our wonderful, mild climate. Because people now live more at the back of the house than the front, it makes perfect sense to extend the living quarters to the outside, in effect making the garden another room.

The pergola has evolved into a semi-enclosed room with a 'floor' that carries a theme in colour and texture from indoors to out. Furniture has advanced beyond the rustic; the old rough-and-ready picnic setting won't do any more. It's been replaced with lightweight, streamlined, all-weather furniture which is able to be moved around the garden. People set aside an area of their garden for

a table and chairs that can be used at any time of the day or night.

Today you might exercise in a lap pool or indulge your senses in a spa. You may have a Zen-inspired reflection pool. The traditional free-form swimming pool puts a strain on limited space, whereas the simple geometric symmetry of the modern lap pool makes this 'water feature' both easier to accommodate and to visually connect to the house.

The spirit of experimentation is alive and well in today's entertaining garden. Elegant urns and pots containing sculptural plants are used as part of the 'green' architecture to screen off private areas. The garden is dressed for special occasions, and cleverly illuminated at night to accentuate pathways and highlight focal >

< points. You lay a table outdoors with the same flair as you would do a dining table indoors. Portable gas heaters manufactured for exterior use provide warmth and mood in the same way that open fires do in the living room.

Barbecue design has gone from basic to bountiful. The simple grill, hibachi and portable Weber have made way for the custom-designed built-in stainless steel outdoor kitchen. The design of today's barbecue makes cooking a breeze and eating outdoors nothing short of a gourmet experience.

These days, kids – and pets – play at ease in the garden alongside their parents who can relax, chat with friends, attend to garden chores, or take some exercise.

SIZE DOESN'T MATTER

Since many houses today take up 75 per cent of the block on which they stand, and as people become space-critical, particularly in the cities, gardens are naturally becoming smaller. Today's entertaining gardens are focusing more on hard landscaping, and paving outstrips lawn in popularity. Gardeners want low-maintenance surfaces and plants that look great all through the year.

Our lifestyles have changed, but our dreams endure – we still want the lemon tree and the shed. Today, though, the lemon tree is likely to be a small potted citrus contained in a Balinese urn and positioned on the deck. And the shed may be a modern storage bay, specifically designed for recycling bins and designer gardening tools.

Furnished with built-in sofas, silk awnings and brightly coloured cushions, entertaining gardens are places well able to adapt to the demands of modern life. Called on to be a venue for a party one day, the next they are transformed into a peaceful retreat where the cares of life can be forgotten as you splash around in the swimming pool with your children.

POOLSIDE DINING

There's nothing quite like entertaining around a pool. It conjures up that feeling of being at a holiday resort. Intimate dinners, family barbecues, kids' pool parties; it's all about a lifestyle choice. Whether you have a lap pool, family-sized pool, reflective pond or simply a water feature, dedicate an area close by, preferably on a flat paved surface, for entertaining where views and sounds of the water can be enjoyed. Here, the pool decking has been dressed for a spicy soirée after sundown. A quick shuffle of accessories and this oriental-style table can be transformed with a setting to suit any occasion. Be sure to use unbreakable tableware and punctuate your theme with fresh flowers on the table or hung as garlands in the trees.

THE DOS AND DON'TS OF POOL SAFETY

DO adhere to pool safety fencing regulations in your area. Contact your local council for details. In essence, every swimming pool should be fenced from the house, so there is no direct access for small children.
DON'T leave the pool gate propped open – ever. A child can lose consciousness within 30 seconds of falling into the water.
DO choose a non-slip surface for pool paving, coping and decking.
DON'T forget sun safety – ensure there is some shade around your pool.
DO entertain safely: don't use glass, which, if broken, can be almost impossible to find in water; don't use

any mains-operated appliances (such as CD players) anywhere near water.
DON'T take anything for granted: take a course to learn resuscitation and place an instruction chart in a prominent position near the pool.
DO store pool chemicals in a safe place: cool, dry, well-ventilated and inaccessible to children.
DON'T store pool chemicals too close together or near domestic chemicals such as pesticides or turps.
DO wear heavy plastic gloves and safety goggles whenever you handle pool chemicals.
DON'T take your eyes off children when they're near the water.

THE SUNROOM

During the 1950s and 1960s, the sunroom was a glorified sleep-out; today it has evolved into something more sophisticated, with purposes ranging from home office or teenager's pad to a casual meals area. Here, the perfect all-seasons room, with its terracotta walls and solid granite table, keeps the home's Tuscan mood. Dark sandstone for the floor cuts down on glare, while classic Lloyd Loom wicker chairs provide comfortable seating. Retractable canvas awnings shade the area on hot days.

TIPS FOR PLANNING A PARTY OUTDOORS

● A theme will give your party an identity. Go for something unusual that will get people talking and create a buzz. For instance, turn your balcony or backyard into a casbah. Use hot pink and orange table-runners and cushions; stake flares around the garden or hang paper lanterns on string across a table.

● You don't need big bucks to host a successful party. If your budget is modest, choose a simple theme, get friends to help with catering or buy platters from the local deli and shop at markets for flowers and fruit – you'll save a fortune.

● If you're using candles, use lots. A hundred tea lights will seem like a sparkling extravagance to your guests, but they cost next to nothing. Put them into little glass votives, inexpensive drinking glasses or in sand-filled brown paper bags.

● Play up 'the garden' as a theme. Use new garden tools as salad servers and spread large leaves over tables, with potted herbs as centrepieces. String patio plants with fairy lights and use a wheelbarrow filled with ice for cold drinks.

● Look after your guests' comfort and enjoyment from the moment they arrive. Keep an area inside the house for coats and handbags. Be mindful of security: don't leave valuables unattended at the front of the house near an open door.

● Make sure your guests know where the bathroom is located, and stock it up with plenty of fresh towels, toilet paper rolls and soaps for their convenience.

● If you're organising seating for guests while they're eating, it's friendlier to set up several little tables; better than trying to fit everyone around one big table.

● Nothing beats the energy of a live performance. However, there has to be a hook-up with power. Be wary of a million electrical cords running from house to garden. The volume will be difficult to control. And remember that the police can shut down the show without warning, no matter what time of day.

10 RULES FOR POOLS

1 Have an idea of what you want. The design of your pool should suit the architecture of your home and your landscaping, if any.
2 Choose a good, reputable builder – this could be the single factor that differentiates a dream pool installation from a nightmare.
3 Interview and get written quotes from at least three pool builders before you make a decision. Check that their licences and insurances are valid, if required in your State.
4 Make sure the written quote includes everything that you discuss with the builder, from the pool's dimensions to included extras, such as underwater lights.
5 Shop around for finance.
6 Enter into a contract with your builder, again with everything outlined in writing. Ask for a standard contract that has some form of industry recognition.
7 Building regulations vary from area to area, but you must have council approval as well as a formal permit from your water authority before work begins.
8 Check the builder's insurances are valid – yes, again, if necessary.
9 Organise to have your new pool covered under your insurance.
10 Ensure the pool company advises on operation and maintenance procedures before the final handover.

A garden that can be used for entertaining and play involves serious planning and an emphasis on function rather than form. In other words, it's more about having the most comfortable seating and less about a showy plant display. But we're not just talking about moving the indoor furniture outside. The best outdoor rooms offer a designated place for sitting and eating, where natural elements provide the structure around which the decorative touches work.

the entertaining garden

AT GROUND LEVEL

Look at the overall picture before you focus on the details. Think about how you want the space to work and how to make the very best use of it.

How often do you entertain? Do you need a large entertaining area, or simply a place to eat with friends and family? Do you want a place to work outside? What about storage for the recycling bins, ladder and mulch? What about a fireplace or built-in barbecue? Be realistic. There's no point in building a gourmet outdoor kitchen if you only intend to use the barbecue once a month.

Decide on the best place for all of your entertaining and relaxing activities in the same way as you would plan your kitchen or living room. You need to allocate specific zones for working, eating, playing, reading and relaxing.

Once these priorities are fixed, it'll be much easier to figure out the layout of your garden. After you've determined the main traffic zones, you can decide where you want the plants to go. Within this framework, you can transform the space into a wonderful entertaining garden that will be used not only in the warmer summer months but all year round. (For more detailed information on the practicalities of planning a garden from the ground up, see page 86.)

THE TRANSITION ZONE

This is the area that physically connects the house to the garden. When planning your garden, look indoors as well. Note which rooms and windows offer the principal views outside and where the main access into the garden will be – orientation is everything.

The progression from inside to out should be fluid. One of the reasons why so many people renovate the back of their house and subsequently install vast window walls of glass is to make that connection with the outdoors obvious. Usually this overlapping space has a hard surface, such as paving, but it could be >

THE EATING AREA

The ability to extend the hours of your day into the garden can constitute the perfect antidote to a busy working life. At the weekend, of course, the garden is the ideal place to forget about time, have a few friends around and relax. Get your priorities right. If you have lunch parties and cook for a crowd like these owners do, make sure the table is big enough to seat everyone. The furniture is placed on a level paved surface handy to the barbecue, yet open to the garden. Sheltered under an established Japanese maple, the 'outdoor room' is a comfortable distance from the house. Framing the space are fragrant ground covers and low-growing shrubs, such as clipped box, planted around the soft-coloured stone paving, while masses of low maintenance perennials, such as euphorbias, and flowering azaleas and rhododendrons fill in the mid level.

< extended as timber decking. If your block is flat, try to add extra visual interest by creating a change of level. A single step into the garden makes a big difference to the perspective. This terraced area can be bonded in style to that of the house, either through reflecting the architecture or with the use of colour. For instance, you could extend the colour of the interior to the outdoors by painting a boundary wall or screen in the same shade. You can also echo the colour and texture of a floor covering, such as carpet, with similarly coloured outdoor pavers or pebbles.

In certain situations you can take advantage of a flat, open, transition space. Think about whether you need it as a safe play area for toddlers (on tricycles) or as an outdoor dining room. Perhaps both? There should be shelter either under a fabric canopy, roofed pergola or verandah, which reinforces the primary function of this transition space as an entrée to your entertaining garden.

SURFACES

An entertaining garden is a subtle partnership between hard landscaping, decorative elements and the plants. Hard surfaces are used to give your garden flow (paths, plateaus) and serviceability. Combined with soft surfaces (earth, sand, water, grass, bark chips), they create the ebb and flow that draws the eye along a line to a focal point.

You can alter the character of each area of the garden by identifying it with a different paving material. This results in a chequerboard pattern at ground level. Restraint and simplicity are the key: avoid too many patterns as it will kill the effect you're trying to achieve.

The durability of a surface will determine its use in the entertaining garden.
Paving: A better solution than grass for the outdoor eating area (be it an extension of the inside living space, or elsewhere in the garden) because, with constant wear, the grass becomes wet >

THE BARBECUE

The good old Aussie ritual of the 'barbie out the back' continues, but the design of today's barbecue makes cooking a breeze and eating outdoors a gourmet experience. This built-in barbecue is safely tucked away in a designated outdoor eating area (opposite). Shrubs and dense massed plantings help integrate the structure into the landscape.

THE POOL FENCE

It's mandatory to install a pool fence and important to choose a design that complements the style of pool. In this garden, a traditional metal pool fence demarcates the swimming zone (below). The landscape designer has created separate activity areas for a sports-loving family in this Melbourne backyard and the pool area doubles as a second entertaining space.

< and muddy as it gets worn down. Avoid gravel and pebbles here as they'll find their way into your shoes, and small children's mouths. Paving is appropriate also for around the barbecue, fish pond, swimming pool and for garden paths. The choice of paving depends on your garden style: tile, marble and stone are more formal than brick and slate. Concrete has an urban edge. Be inventive and mix materials for a 'dressy' effect; this not only looks good but often provides a better foothold anyway.

Pebbles and gravel: These surfaces give exciting textural interest and can be fashioned into any design. When space is tight, as in an urban garden or courtyard, use bright white pebbles for their light-reflecting quality in a border or to replace grass. Polished black pebbles add a dramatic touch when laid to highlight

a sculptural plant. Gravel helps keep the weeds in check, which makes it suitable for areas which require minimal maintenance, such as the recycling bay and under the clothesline.

Decking: Timber decking is especially good for main traffic areas and where you need to make a smooth transition between levels. It can be installed as a raised 'floating' floor over uneven surfaces and gives natural softness underfoot.

PRIVACY AND SHADE

Shade, shelter and privacy give the entertaining garden its versatility. The pergola, once used only as a lightweight vine arbour or 'walk-through' offering shade as well as support for plants, has come into its own. Constructed in either timber or metal, the pergola is usually planted with a deciduous climber, such as ornamental >

THE MODERN LOGGIA
The traditional pool house these days gives way to an elegant open-sided loggia, a Mediterranean-inspired roofed structure that provides shade and enclosure for poolside dining and lounging. This chic hotel-style pool (above) is complemented in style with a loggia that also offers a respite to weary tennis players coming off the court below.

ALL-WEATHER FURNITURE
In our climate it's imperative to choose your outdoor furniture to suit the conditions. The owners here have opted for all-weather wicker (opposite). Plants are equally low maintenance and include a snowball bush in full bloom and clumps of dietes under cypress pruned of their lower branches.

YEAR-ROUND LIVING
The way indoor/outdoor living works is to have seamless boundaries. Critical to the overall success of the effect is the marriage of materials. A great example is seen here in this Adelaide house. Oversized pavers of unpolished travertine extend the living area out to the walled courtyard with its terraced, Greek-style garden beds, filled with potted cycads, clipped ficus, ivy and ragged clumps of mondo grass. Imposing double-height glass panels afford a dynamic perspective from inside. A counter-top with built-in barbecue, fridge and sink allows the terrace to function as an outdoor kitchen, truly creating a beautiful zone for year-round living.

< grape or wisteria, which provides a dense cover for shade in summer but allows light through in winter. A pergola might have a roof of clear polycarbonate, fine metal mesh or pencil-thin bamboo sheeting to extend its life as a semi-enclosed outdoor room.

Shade and privacy treatments vary enormously in contemporary gardens, from stretched canvas and glass frames, Asian-inspired slatted wood screens, muslin-curtained tents and lattice screens, to canvas sails and canopies. Market umbrellas provide temporary shade and shelter to eating areas and around the swimming pool. Modern weatherproof fabrics, which resist mould, mildew and chlorine, are available in dozens of exciting designs and colours,

but canvas still remains popular. Tough marine sailcloth is also used for sail canopies. Remember that sails and canopies must be securely anchored by ropes or wires either into the ground or at fixed points on the exterior wall.

GARDEN FURNITURE

These days, the style of modern garden furniture replicates what you have in your living room. The natural look is skilfully imitated in such contemporary materials as fibreglass, poly resins, aluminium and industrial stainless steel, however, traditional teak, Australian hardwoods and weatherproof wicker are still popular. Chairs and tables have a sculptural quality; the rustic colour palette of yesterday has given way to cool neutrals, smart >

THE FAMILY GARDEN

Kids and dogs are not obviously compatible with gardens. They'll dig holes, throw balls, roll on the grass, fall into your favourite plants... and that's just the children! There are ways, however, to make their relationship with your garden run a little more smoothly.

● Avoid rare and exotic plants – it's these that children invariably fall on or 'pick for mummy'. It's best to stick to cheap and cheerful plants until your children have passed toddlerhood (1). With dogs, you may need to keep your 'easy-care' plant collection a lot longer.

● The best way to ensure that your children respect the garden is to involve them (2). Give them an area to call their own and encourage them to grow what interests them. Children love plants they can eat, so why not try a vegie garden, with cherry tomatoes, strawberries, lettuces, radishes and parsley?

● A sandpit (3) is invaluable for children or puppies. Both love to dig, and better they do it there than in your garden beds! The ideal sandpit is made with treated pine logs, a porous liner to separate sand and soil, a load of sandpit sand, a cover to keep out cats and rain, and some sort of shade above.

● Give them a hard-wearing lawn on which to play, perhaps in a tent (4) or cubby house (5). Try kikuyu, perennial rye or tall fescue. Whichever type you choose, ensure you aerate your lawn with a garden fork at least once a year, to break up soil compacted under endless games.

< greys and white. A stone or timber bench is often included as a resting point at the end of a path, or as a safe and stable seat for children. Seating built or recessed into a wall or deck is a solution for small gardens. When selecting furniture, choose comfort over appearance.

CHILD'S PLAY

Children need somewhere to play, even in the most sophisticated garden. For the under-fours a sandpit is mandatory (down the track this can be turned into a water feature). When it's not in use, keep it covered against straying animals and wet weather. Most play equipment in the shops is gaudy, bulky and expensive. Instead, why not choose timber as the material for a cubby, tree-house or swing? Lay rubber pads or thick mulch under the swing to soften heavy landings.

Paths can double as little cycling tracks for trikes and bikes, so choose your surfaces carefully. A basketball hoop on a hard surface is a good idea for older children. A rectangle of grass will work well for cricket, boules or other ball games.

If a pet is part of your family, include a paved corner for its equipment (paving is easy to hose down). Avoid a lot of grass and fragile flower beds; dogs will dig them up. Small children find loose pebbles, stones and gravel fascinating to pop into their mouths, and so these surfaces can be a safety hazard. Think twice about their use in the garden when your children are very young.

IN THE SWIM

Not every garden has the space for a swimming pool, but a decorative water feature is always possible. In a garden for entertaining, the sound of trickling water can be a great joy. More people these days are seeing the merit in having a lap pool for exercise; the narrow width makes it less intrusive in the backyard landscape than a larger free-form style of pool. The pool's reflective qualities are an added bonus, too. Note that the darkest pools give the sharpest reflections. The traditional bright turquoise tiles (which look rather alien in all but the flashiest resort swimming pools) do not merge into their surroundings as well as the more subtle dark greens and navy blues.

Low planting around the pool and a high water line create eye-line reflections, which swimmers will enjoy. Any pool has its dangers for the very young and a pool fence must be included at the initial design stage. Avoid areas covered with loose pebbles and gravel near the pool. >

3 4

5 6

7 8

EXTENDING DAY INTO NIGHT

Exterior lighting performs several functions, depending on its positioning within the garden. In the front garden, pathways must be brightly lit to provide safe access; a warm, welcoming light should be positioned near the front door, highlighting your property number; and security lighting, which detects movement, can alert you to the presence of intruders (or, it must be said, cats!). In other areas of the garden, uplights can be used to highlight a feature tree, downlights to draw attention to a beautiful statue, and underwater lights to provide a spectacular evening display. For entertaining, consider the use of bud or fairy lights, or lanterns and candles for atmosphere, though you will need more permanent lighting, such as fixed, low-voltage luminaries, to ensure you can cook outdoors and guests can see what they're eating. A selection of these will work better than one fixed bright light. *As the sun sets, your outdoor entertaining area takes on a completely different look. Colours alter, the mood swings, the tempo slows, then, under night lights, it comes alive again. On these pages are examples of lighting plans integrated into the overall garden design concept.* **1 & 2** *Shaped topiary trees take on a theatrical guise and the pool's life is extended.* **3 & 4** *Seating becomes a romantic hideaway.* **5 & 6** *Fountains and pools look dramatic when illuminated.* **7 & 8** *Night lighting accentuates the shape and line of architectural features and makes trickling fountains sparkle.*

OUTDOOR COOKING

Our weather is conducive to cooking up a storm outdoors. But it can fizzle or sizzle depending on how you gear up. Decide what you prefer to cook and how often. Portable is best if you're not a frequent barbecuer. If the focus of your outdoor entertaining is oven-cooked food, consider something more permanent in the way of a built-in gourmet kitchen. Wood-fired pizzas and bread are popular and they taste all the better when made outdoors. This solid brick, flued, wood-fired pizza oven is simple to incorporate into your entertaining garden. The oven takes four to five hours to heat, but cooks pizzas in minutes.

< CHOOSING THE PLANTS

Our attitude to gardening has changed as the demands on our time become greater. People want low-maintenance gardens, especially if they are in constant use for outdoor entertaining. Who wants to prune, mulch and hose when the sunshine beckons and friends are about to arrive for lunch in the garden?

There is a huge emphasis on instant gardens with plants that can be contained in urns, pots and gravel-topped beds. Fewer plants are put in the garden but those which are planted are chosen for their dramatic effect. Plants are also selected for their colourful foliage. And at last people are acknowledging our climate in a way that sees low-maintenance native species used to create focal points, screen corners and camouflage utility structures such as the garage and the shed.

You might think more about the size that a tree will reach, rather than just planting any species on a whim. Decorative grasses, such as mondo grass, and flowering herbs, such as chamomile and thyme, are often combined with hard landscaping to create a pathway, patio or private corner that's both original in style and aromatic to walk on.

FURNITURE FOR OUTDOORS

Unless you're going to keep your outdoor furniture undercover or in a storeroom, it will need to be able to withstand the rigours of our climate. You have essentially five different materials from which to choose; each adds a different look to your garden, and each requires its own particular brand of maintenance.

Timber: Teak is the best timber for outdoor furniture because it doesn't splinter and lasts almost forever, fading to a soft, silver-grey (**1**). Oiling it regularly will help it to retain a brown finish. Other hardwoods and softwoods such as pine can be painted, but otherwise should be oiled or stained regularly to maintain the finish and quality of the timber.

Stone: For permanence, you can't go past stone, which weathers well and is easy to clean (**2**). While the colour can blend beautifully into the garden, stone furniture is heavy and difficult to move. Probably best in most cases for a feature seat rather than a full outdoor table setting.

Metal: For European-style sophistication, consider metal (**3**). Aluminium, steel and forged iron are all options for outdoors, but they must be treated to ensure they don't rust. Aluminium is powder-coated for protection and comes in many colours.

Plastics: Moulded polypropylene is the most popular type of outdoor furniture because it comes in styles and shapes to suit almost every type of garden and budget. It's lightweight and easy to move around, and can simply be hosed off.

Cane/wicker: This is best suited to a covered patio or deck, unless you opt for all-weather wicker, which is made from steel-reinforced, fine woven fibre that's finished with a spray of UV-rated paint.

POOLSIDE

Plants that grow around a swimming pool have very special requirements. First and foremost, they need to be tough, as they are often expected to grow in full sun next to hot paving. They also need to be manageable and to provide privacy. Plants that are evergreen and can be clipped, shaped and pruned meet these two requirements. Poolside plants should also be safe to be around. Don't select any with thorns or sharp spines; avoid plants that attract lots of bees; avoid those with small flowers, leaves or needles that may fall into the water and block pool pumps; and watch out for any that could cause an allergic reaction. Remember also to choose plants that will be in flower when the pool is in use.

1. Orthrosanthus, with its blue flowers, accentuates the restful tones of the pool and its painted lattice and pergola. A low, clipped juniper hedge borders the far side of the pool.
2. Hydrangea is a deciduous shrub that flowers in summer but needs shade and lots of watering, so use it to provide highlights in among lush shrubs and overshadowing trees. Its flowers can be blue, white, pink or colours in between.
3. Cypress and junipers, with their narrow, upright growth habit, give this pool and dining area year-round privacy.
4. Conifers should be chosen with care, avoiding any with needles. The golden biota (*Thuja orientalis*) pictured here is a popular choice for gardens as it is dense and slow-growing.

5. Bougainvillea, with its vibrant colours, brings a tropical warmth to any garden. In confined areas around a pool, its vigorous growth and thorns can be a problem, so seek out dwarf 'Bambino' bougainvilleas, which can be grown in a pot.
6. Palms are favourite poolside plants but, for shade and privacy, choose low, clumping varieties. Keep them well-watered and mulched with chopped spent fronds.
7. Ferns, such as the bird's nest fern (front), and other foliage plants, such as agave, provide a lush setting for this pool.
8. Pigface (lampranthus) is a low, spreading succulent, one of the all-time low-maintenance plants for a hot dry spot such as near the pool. Expect an electric display of yellow, orange, red,

pink, purple or white flowers in spring and summer.
9. Plumbago 'Royal Cape' is a strong, vibrant, blue-flowered plant that can be clipped into a soft hedge around a pool.
10. Agapanthus, with its blue or white lily flowers on stout stems in summer and mounds of evergreen strappy leaves, makes a natural poolside choice. The clumps look good all year. Dead head flower stalks in late summer before they form seeds. Best in full sun.
11. Hibiscus (*H. rosa-sinensis*) is a great choice to grow around a pool in a warm, frost-free climate. These deciduous shrubs provide months of flower colour from late spring to autumn. Select named varieties by colour and height.

SUCCULENTS

With their ability to cope with wind, harsh sun and extended dry times, succulents are perfectly suited to survive in the exposed conditions of decks and patios. Not only are they incredibly tough, they also look stylish and most are people and pot friendly. Great choices for suburban gardens include the all-purpose *Agave attenuata*, many of the sedums, and the 'can't-kill' jade plants. Jade plants are also said to bring good luck. Where space is limited, collect miniature succulents in interesting pots and make them into miniature gardens. Other plants that are hardy enough to thrive in harsh conditions include the glamorous bromeliads, with their thick leaves and succulent-like growth habit.

1. Sedum, potted here with a backdrop of lavender, has colourful leaves and may also produce stunning flowers. Succulents don't need to be grown in either deep or traditional pots. Use a recycled container as a talking piece and fill it with a free-draining succulent mix, making sure there are ample drainage holes in the base of the container.
2. *Agave attenuata* is a sculptural plant for a large pot or planter. The chief benefit of using this species on a deck or in a confined garden is that it doesn't have sharp spines on the tips of its leaves. Where space permits, a row of these plants in a long container, such as a planter box, can be a stunning choice on a deck.
3. Graptopetalum, combined with blue chalksticks, provides a good contrast of foliage, colour and shape.
4. Cacti and succulents, such as aeonium (back, right), are unified by pot colour – most are grown in terracotta pots of various sizes. Varying the heights of the pots by arranging them on a plant stand also adds to the effect that can be achieved. In the background, the medicinal plant, *Aloe vera* (back, left), is included, grown for its shape as well as its healing powers.
5. Echeverias are displayed inside a recycled metal pot. Where space permits, have other plants on standby, to be moved into the decorative outer pot for a change of scenery.
6. Tall crassulas, leafy flax and low-growing rosette-forming

succulents thrive in groups of pots on a sunny deck. Watch for snails and slugs that may damage foliage, and grow all succulents in a free-draining potting mix.
7. Bromeliads, like this aechmea, are not true succulents, but do share many of the features that make succulents so popular. They come in all shapes and sizes, have showy leaves and produce colourful flowers that last for months. Keep their central well topped up with water.
8. Kalanchoe is an excellent choice for a succulent garden. Here, lavender scallops (*Kalanchoe pumila*) combines colourful leaves and pink spring flowers. It suits a sunny position in cold climates, otherwise it prefers dappled shade.

4

5

TOP TIPS FOR DECKS

Gardens on decks are usually confined to containers, so grow plants to cascade over the pot's edge or provide a fringe of colour. Try black or green mondo grass, parsley, Spanish shawl, convolvulus, nasturtiums and miniature ivy.

The best choices for a hot, windy or salt-breeze-affected deck are plants with small, tough, leathery leaves. Grow them in large, heavy pots to keep them stable – lightweight pots may be blown over.

Apart from succulents, truly tough choices for exposed decks include:

• Rockery gardenia (*Gardenia* 'Radicans').

• NZ Christmas bush, especially dwarf or variegated forms of *Metrosideros kermadecensis*.

• Indian hawthorn; for pink flowers try *Rhaphiolepis* 'Apple Blossom'.

• Weeping figs (*Ficus benjamina*).

• Coprosma in all its forms.

6

7

8

KIDS' BACK GARDEN

Kids love plants that are either edible or curious to look at or to touch. Many kids also like flowering plants that buzz with bees, such as lavender or gaura. And they enjoy plants, such as buddleia or lantana, that attract butterflies. Some kids delight in growing plants that look strange, such as carnivorous plants or bat plants, or that have weird or wacky names like the jellybean plant, a succulent with jellybean-like leaves. The following choices need sun and can be grown in garden beds or in pots. Many of these plants are easy to grow from seed. If you have a shaded garden, encourage the kids to concentrate on impatiens (kids love to pop their explosive seed heads) with a ground cover of native violet, ferns and mosses.

1. Strawberries are easy to grow from small plants or runners and provide a ready harvest in early spring. Give them ample water and a mulch of lucerne to keep the fruit clear of the ground. If necessary, cover the plants with a net to stop birds (and pets) beating the kids to the fruit. For something a little different, look for a new pink-flowered strawberry, 'Bliss', which will fruit throughout the year. Strawberries can also be grown in pots or hanging baskets in a sunny spot.

2. Watering is always a favourite with kids who like to help in the garden. Child-sized watering cans and garden tools are available at many nurseries.

3. Red-hot pokers (*Kniphofia* species) are magnificent in full flower in bold red, orange or yellow. They will attract nectar-loving birds to your garden as well.

4. Sunflowers are easy to grow from seed but are also available as seedlings. Plant in spring in a sunny, sheltered spot such as against a fence. The soil should be dug over and have some compost or well-rotted manure added before planting. There are many named varieties including a double-flowered dwarf form called 'Teddy Bear', but the giant pictured here grows readily from seed.

5. Soft-hearted lettuce varieties such as 'Salad Bowl' can be tucked in anywhere, grow quickly and can be picked whole or a few leaves at a time.

6. Daisies are rewarding shrubs for kids to grow and to pick.

They flower from winter for many months, can be grown from cuttings, and grow quickly to flowering size.

7. Dwarf French marigolds, here combined with white alyssum, are a great choice for kids. Both alyssum and marigolds grow readily from seed or seedling and are not too fussy about soil type. Other good flowering choices to grow from seed include candytuft, sweet peas and nasturtiums.

8. Radishes add an edible dimension to the kids' garden. They are fast-growing vegetables, which can be started from seed. There are many other fruits and vegies that can be grown easily: try cherry tomatoes, carrots, mandarins, parsley, passionfruit, rocket and snow peas.

An authentic Balinese pavilion is the centrepoint of this lush Queensland garden, designed to give its owners a permanent reminder of their favourite holiday destination.

influences

inspire

Australian gardens reflect the diversity of Australian society today. British influences may have been the starting point of our gardening traditions, but the 20th century layered new inspirations over our roots. As our ties to Asia have strengthened, so too has our attachment to bamboo, Zen ideals and water features. Waves of immigration have brought horticultural practices and lifestyle revelations from Italy, Greece, China, Vietnam and more. Now we have access to colours, plants and design ideas from sources as diverse as India and Morocco, France and Mexico. Best of all, they're as close as your nursery and all you need is a plan.

BALINESE TROPICAL

Essence: Wet tropical gardens are exuberant with lush, bold foliage, large-leafed plants and water features.

Architecture: Pavilion, stone embellishments, Hindu shrines.

Features: Carved figures in stone or timber benches and fretwork, wind chimes, large urns and containers.

Plants: Palms, plants with strap-like leaves and those with bold or coloured foliage predominate. The range of tropical plants is huge and barely touched in warm climate Australia. Even in cooler areas, it is possible to find plants which are cold adapted but give the look of lush foliage and abundant moisture without water-guzzling habits.

Colour: Mostly green with splashes of vibrant colour from tropical flowering plants and variegated or coloured foliage. Red, orange and yellow are the most prominent colours with white and green variegated foliage.

Step into the garden at Suan Sawan in Queensland and you're in a subtropical paradise. The owners love wandering in the rainforest so they've re-created their own in their backyard. With its swaying palms, lush stems sprouting from still waters, and Balinese pavilion – known as a bale – it's hard to believe this is Australia! The block of land is small and visitors go on a journey from 'mountains' through to 'jungle' to a tea room on a 'lake'. Plant groupings and pebble paths define the different areas which each have a small sculpture, pot pond or timber spirit house.

AUSTRALIAN COASTAL

Essence: Designed to suit and confront the elements head-on, the garden thrives in spite of salt spray, strong winds and poor, sandy soils.

Architecture: Buildings evocative of a coastal lifestyle can be of natural timber highlighted by greyish green or blue paintwork. Exotic seaside gardens can be bright and breezy, emboldened with primary and hot colours.

Features: Windswept plants, leathery leaves, gravel to imitate sand, local stone outcrops, found objects such as driftwood, shells or weathered rock, with views of water or ocean. Sculptural elements usually have some connection to water, such as representations of sea birds, shipping artefacts or abstract works of rusted metal.

Plants: Low ground-hugging plants that take salt spray such as *Acacia, Correa, Banksia* and *Melaleuca* species, coast rosemary and *Hibiscus tiliaceus.*

Colour: Foliage is mostly subdued grey-greens with occasional colour breaks, such as the bronze or burgundy foliage on *Agonis* 'After Dark' or the purple forms of hibiscus.

A series of dry creek beds meander down this hillside, at Palm Beach, NSW, crisscrossing pathways in amongst viewing landings and retaining walls. After losing many plants to the coastal elements, the owner has found the best performers to be melaleucas, Banksia robur, grevilleas, tea-trees and lillypillies. The 250 or so plants are approaching their third season of survival and the owner prunes them a little at a time, using the analogy that, in the wild, fauna nibbles the tops off plants. They need little water and the plantings follow the natural contours of the landscape, with large rocky outcrops – some forming natural terraces – adding contrast and drama.

SANTA FE STYLE

Essence: Bright colours and a sun-washed, outdoorsy feel, usually with dry-adapted plants and earthy clay or terracotta urns and pots. It's a sunny style, ideal for dry summer climates and desert locations.

Architecture: Free-form adobe walls either painted with neutral limewashes or brighter shades, heavy timbered doors with feature hinges and natural weathered timber often in a Spanish mission style. Heavy exposed beams often feature.

Features: Borrows heavily from two traditions: one Spanish, the other Pueblo Indian. Patterns reflect Indian blanket designs and desert artefacts.

Plants: Any plants adapted to hot, dry summers and cold winters are fine. Rudbeckias, sunflowers, arctotis, shasta and other daisies are good, as are the vast array of succulents.

Colour: The combinations are important. If walls are neutral, use bright colours to accent timberwork on windows, seats or doors. Fabric covers, cushions and umbrellas add extra vibrancy. If walls are bright, tone down flowering plants with greater emphasis on foliage shape and colours, adding texture with silver, eucalyptus greens and bluish leaves.

A chance meeting between the owner of this house and Californian interior decorator Lynda Kerry brought about this wonderful Sante Fe terrace garden and pool in Sydney. An outdoor dining table in the paved courtyard is where long summer meals are enjoyed. Oversized terracotta urns and masks line the space, while propped cushions make this a place to relax. Rough rendered walls, woven baskets and striped blankets in vivid Pueblo colours are all key components of Santa Fe style, from the American state of New Mexico.

ENGLISH COUNTRY

Essence: Sweeping green lawns, wide borders filled with a mix of perennial flowers and roses.

Architecture: Rustic styling, timber structures with shingled roofs or pergolas used to support climbing plants.

Features: Gazebos and summerhouses, arbours, teak garden benches, with perhaps a dovecote or birdbath.

Plants: Perennials and roses, bulbs in season, irises, plants that mass for colourful display, gravel paths, timber fences.

Colour: Often pastel, with pink predominating, pale yellows and apricots with the contrast of silver and lime foliage.

Copious amounts of horse manure from ponies on this property have made this country garden bloom. Situated in Berry, on the NSW South Coast, this garden is devised around soft pastels. Roses, camellias and every perennial known to man are the owners' favourites and the garden is filled to overflowing. It started out with a formal structure but the owners have let it have its way and it has loosened into a more cottagey affair with lawns connecting flower beds.

SPANISH COURTYARD

Essence: Imagine a hot dry summer's day, olive trees, a formal fountain, some big old olive jars and the strong structure of low hedges. That's the recipe for a Spanish courtyard. You could be in an old Mediterranean monastery garden escaping the daily grind, while enjoying a cooling breeze and the gentle splash of water beneath shady trees.

Architecture: Solid masonry walls often stuccoed with recesses for statues or grilled windows. Arches, loggias and other covered walkways provide a host for billowing vines and shade in summer.

Features: Formal fountains with circular, hexagonal or similarly geometric shapes, often featuring a classical statue or fountainhead.

Plants: Olive trees, shrubs and perennials with silver and grey foliage, plants for clipping such as box and pittosporum, shrubs and vines for colourful highlights like plumbago, bougainvillea, oleanders, and ubiquitous pots and baskets of geraniums.

Colour: Walls painted in earthy colours or neutrals with colourful splashes from flowering plants.

Spanish magic fills the front courtyard of a Brisbane home. A central water feature provides a soft, replenishing energy, its fish pond base filled with waterlilies and sacred lotus; the cupid was found in the original garden. Paths of pale cream gravel and porphyry stone cobbles contrast with the vibrant green of the Japanese box hedges which, in turn, surround silvery grey olive trees. Under the olives, herbs such as marjoram and chives are alternated, and softening the house walls is a thick hedge of Camellia sasanqua. The garden has perfect structure, but nature still flows within.

JAPANESE TRANQUILLITY

Essence: Otherworldly and ethereal, the Japanese garden is possibly the most spiritual of all garden styles. Deeply rooted in Zen Buddhist principles of balance and restraint, self-discipline is essential.

Architecture: Buildings are normally copies of a Japanese teahouse or pagoda-like structures, but the style lends itself to adaptation and rustic and vernacular architectural styles using natural materials can be appropriate.

Features: Lakes and cascades, koi ponds, trees clipped into miniature form to represent great antiquity, granite lanterns and use of pebbles and interestingly shaped rocks to represent mountains and hills. Koi carp may add colour and movement in place of flowers.

Plants: Japanese maples, single-flowered, one-colour azaleas such as the Kurume varieties, *Osmanthus fragrans*, clumping bamboo, mondo grass, *Ardisia crenata*, camellias and many conifers feature in Japanese gardens. In most cases plants are carefully pruned and shaped, often with a symbolic meaning behind the design.

Colour: Mostly green with limited seasonal colour such as a clipped bank of azaleas, autumn berries or deciduous leaves. The Japanese garden is never a riot of colour but a quiet reflective place with a restrained spiritual ambience.

The distinct Oriental personality of this Canberra garden is harnessed by bold, clipped shapes (which depict the mountainous terrain of Japan), contrasting textures and, of course, a shallow-water pond with a tiny waterfall. Planted alongside tree ferns, pebbles and rocks are azaleas and junipers; in Japanese gardens the shape, texture and placement of rocks and stones is vitally important. A studied arrangement of pebbles surrounding a water bowl (above) is a Sanzan grouping (a Japanese tri-stone garden feature) representing the trilogy of heaven, earth and man. Azaleas are traditional choices in a Japanese garden, as are the granite icons subtly introduced into this beautiful setting.

MOROCCAN MAGIC

Essence: Heir to the Moorish gardens of the Arabs and the Persian 'paradise' gardens, Moroccan style is a creature of a hot, dry climate. Palms, fruit trees and flowering fragrant shrubs tantalise the senses.

Architecture: Typically Moorish, with arches, carved doors and stonework; masonry walls enclosing a formal garden of gravel paths and rectangular ponds and rills (narrow water channels) representing the irrigation canals of the desert.

Features: Intricate glass and metal lanterns, wirework grilles and hidden windows. Tiled tables and wrought-iron chairs add to the visual experience.

Plants: Citrus, large succulents such as dragon's blood tree (*Dracaena draco*), aeonium, yuccas or aloes, bougainvillea, geraniums, sun-hardy flowers like daylilies, agapanthus, plumbago or oleander, dwarf date or phoenix palms and dry-adapted plants such as echium, cork oak and olive.

Colour: The colour most associated with Moroccan gardens is Majorelle blue, named after the French artist, Louis Majorelle. It is expensive because of the cobalt used in its manufacture. Walls in buff, cream or light apricot are acceptable alternatives. Salmon pink and other warm pastels are common against green or greyish foliage, while blue flowers are cooling in summer. The occasional bright red bloom from hibiscus or bougainvillea provides a vivid contrast with Majorelle blue.

This deceptively spacious courtyard has been given an Eastern flavour by Sydney designer Bridget Tyer. The cream-based scheme creates a sense of calm, and honed limestone tiles flow through from the living area into the courtyard's lower terrace. Tuscan stone pavers, edged with mondo grass, feature on the upper level and an Indian wedding chest has become a seat. Clay lanterns adorn the walls for night-time use and terracotta pots top the rear wall.

creating the best design

The fun part of creating a garden is that you really can design an imaginative outdoor world. It's your own personal space and should reflect your interests, passions and any cultural references you choose to include. Your backyard can be a little corner of a Pacific island or even a serene, Japanese-inspired courtyard. You can sunbake on your Mediterranean-style terrace or relax under a garland of roses in an English cottage garden. It's up to you. You pick the style of your wildest dreams and aspirations, then let colours, plants, paving and decorations do the rest.

FORMULATING A PLAN

No matter what garden style you've selected, the groundwork necessary to translate your great ideas into a back garden is the same. First comes the research: look at magazines, books, nurseries, the internet, seed catalogues, other people's gardens. As your thoughts and ideas begin to take shape, don't be tempted to reach for a chainsaw or a spade. Instead, put pencil to paper.

Start by assessing what's in the garden already, why it is there, what can be removed, and what you'd like to add.

Even if you don't want to create an elaborate plan, at least do some sketches that will help illustrate your ideas as you talk to a professional garden designer.

Think about the future. You may not be able to afford the extension and the pool now, but at least consider where they'll go and plan and plant accordingly. You don't want to have to move plants to make way for other items such as the clothesline, barbecue, deck or the kids' swings. The spot for the future swimming pool or tennis court isn't the place to plant a graceful shade tree. A few years down the track, when the tree is in the way, it'll need council approval and an expensive tree surgeon to take it away.

CHECKING THE SITE

Begin with a copy of the scale plan for your property, along with a pencil and a measuring tape. Use a photocopy, not the original house plans.

Find a fixed point, such as the boundary lines or the house, and measure all the features that exist in the yard so they can be noted on the plan. These will include existing trees (measure not only where they are but also how far their branches spread and show this on the plan as a circle), paths, steps and paving.

Note problem areas that need fixing, such as hot areas that need shading, open areas that need screening for privacy, and sloping sections that need steps or levelling. Work out where the sunny and shady spots are, and where the breezes and strong winds come from.

If they're not already on the plan, carefully mark all the services such as gas, phone, electricity and drainage. These are obstacles to avoid at all costs.

All the measurements you make out-doors need to be converted to scale. Plans are usually 1:50, 1:100 or 1:200 but the information will be included in the key.

The easiest scale to work to is 1:100, as it means that 1cm on your plan will equal one metre in your garden. For example, a swimming pool would measure about 10 metres long by three metres across; at 1:100 scale, the pool would be 10 centimetres long by three centimetres across.

Most plans also identify which direction is north. If this is missing, use a compass and mark it on your plan – knowing the aspect of your garden is vital when it comes to plant selection.

PUTTING IT TOGETHER

If you're calling in professional advice, now's the time to get on the phone. If you're a DIY aficionado, this is the stage where you allocate space to all the important things you need to include within the space that's available. Play around with different ideas and combinations to make sure that you've developed a workable plan. An easy way to do this is to put tracing paper over your site plan and work on the tracing. To try another combination of ideas, simply add a new piece of tracing paper.

Always work in a soft pencil with a rubber handy to allow for changing your mind. You can even create your plan on your computer using readily available software packages.

Some of the things to include on your >

FRENCH PROVINCIAL

Essence: Think summer, country styling and weathered wire furniture and accessories. An eclectic style that's relaxed with highly structured elements.

Architecture: Buildings are often rustic with stone and rendered walls. Structures may include arbours and pergolas laden with wisteria or roses.

Features: Aged terracotta pots housing topiary trees or shrubs are common elements. Crushed granite paths and terraces make a good place to sit containers close to the house. Further from the building, the garden becomes more relaxed.

Plants: The classic foliage and culinary plants are lavender, rosemary and bay, but for summer think also of iris, easy-to-grow nasturtiums and lax, spreading erigeron or seaside daisy. For colour, add banks of dahlias blended with wispy perennials like gaura and old-fashioned roses.

Colour: Soft greys, blues, pinks, rich greens, deep wines and berries, all reflecting the verdant French countryside.

A tiny inner-city Sydney courtyard features well-chosen plants that are elegant and fragrant, yet simple to upkeep. Star jasmine, camellia espaliered on the rendered wall, ficus, lavender, 'Iceberg' roses and rosemary all create the modern French provincial look.

CHINESE PAVILION

Essence: A garden to stroll in and explore. It often meanders around a large water feature or an artificial lake with specimen trees and seasonal plantings.

Architecture: The traditional garden features a cluster of buildings – teahouse, pagoda and viewing pavilions ornamented with decorative tiles and timber fretwork – linked by covered walkways.

Features: Cascades of water, rocky outcrops representing mountains, informal paths,

bridges, walls with moon gate entrances and glazed ceramic sculptures or large ornate pots.

Plants: Usually Chinese in origin with maples, camellias, bamboo, mondo grass, azaleas and peonies in cooler areas, and hibiscus, lotus and allamanda in warm zones.

Colour: Seasonal displays of flowering plants to invoke contemplation.

Traditional Chinese gardens are based on Yin and Yang, the contrast of light and shade, small and large, rough and

smooth. Water is an essential element, often surrounded by rocks and beautiful timber pagodas. Here, in this miniature Chinese garden, a Japanese maple sits over a central pond, etched with rocks of the palest grey. The main building is surrounded by cypress trees and Camellia sasanqua are planted alongside a miniature peach tree. A classical zigzag bridge (traditionally built to deter spirits) spans the fish pond and a small pavilion is set up for a game of chess.

< plan are space to grow plants, space to relax, and space for children or pets to play. You also need room for utilities, such as compost heaps, rubbish bins and a clothesline, and perhaps for parking and storage. As you work on your plan, think about what your layout will look like from inside the house. You don't really want garbage bins or the compost heap in front of the living room windows.

THINK ABOUT THESE SPACES

● Utility spaces. Every garden needs space set aside for the clothesline, the compost heap, the tool shed and rubbish bin storage. These utilitarian areas need to be accessible, but not on view. For clothes drying, the line should be in the sun.

● Outdoor dining. Look at sun and shade and proximity to the kitchen. Work out where the shade from trees and buildings falls during the time of day you are most likely to eat or cook outdoors. If shade isn't there when needed, include a pergola or other form of protection. Allow room for a table, chairs and a barbecue.

● Relaxing spaces. Every garden needs somewhere to relax. This may be a spot to get away from it all, screened from the house, or it could be somewhere to sit just near the house. You'll want shade here, too, and something to look at.

● Space for the kids. Kids want lots of entertainment in a garden. Position the children's play areas for safety, for example within view of the kitchen window. Also, consider some shade, either from a tree or a specially erected shade sail. The play areas may not be permanent as children's needs change as they grow.

● Garden beds. Plants are easiest to care for when they're grouped in beds. Rather than allocate single plants, think of making larger spaces for garden beds. For herbs or vegetables, make sure some garden beds are in the sunniest spot.

● Trees. Make provision for growing at least one tree, preferably more if the garden is large enough. Plant trees where they will offer shade and shelter but not be so close to the house or fence that they cause problems (at least three metres away from walls is preferred).

● Lawn. Lawn areas should be in the sunny parts of the garden. Avoid creating small, fragmented lawns as these are hard to mow and maintain.

● Swimming pool and spa. If either or both of these are a long-term goal, leave or allocate space on your plan. Also make sure that the site you've set aside is accessible for tradespeople and equipment. Don't plant a large tree in the area reserved for the pool, however it could be the spot for the vegetable garden, sand pit, lawn, or a flower garden that are all easy to relocate in the future.

● Pond and water features. Site water features where you can see or hear them, and near a power source. In a large space, place the water feature at the lowest point, where water might gather naturally.

MEDITERRANEAN

Essence: The true Mediterranean garden pays homage to the sun and its bounties. It is about enjoyment and the pleasures of the plate – sun-ripened fruit, bread and olive oil in surroundings of shady bowers and colourful flowers.

Architecture: Pergolas, arches and protected areas for outdoor living are de rigeur. Grow vines for shade and add a barbecue or an outdoor pizza oven.

Features: Include a large paved area for social gatherings, with a refectory-style table for relaxed get-togethers with family and friends. Use large urns or terracotta containers for specimen shrubs or the long-term flowers of geraniums from spring to autumn, when the garden is most used.

Plants: Grow a grapevine over the pergola for shade and maybe a bougainvillea in a sunny dry spot. On the boundaries, lemons and other citrus, either in pots or in the ground, could be complemented by fruiting trees such as fig, mulberry, pomegranate or apricot. Add perfume with gardenia, yellow ginger, angel's trumpet or cherry pie.

Colour: Blue and yellow shades spring instantly to mind, with a smattering of white or red geraniums as highlights.

The Italian Renaissance introduced symmetry to garden design by dividing spaces and creating 'rooms'. Here, in this Melbourne garden, geometrical shapes come from clipped parterre and topiary while a strong sense of enclosure is derived from high walls and overhanging trees. The Roman archway, edifices and huge potted urns add the vertical walls component. The 'floor' is blond pebble and sandstone.

CONSERVATORIES

Light, space and warmth in winter: the old-fashioned idea of a conservatory is suddenly very modern indeed. While those in the northern States of Australia probably find little of interest in the idea, preferring instead to create screened, shaded areas, those in more temperate climes will find the idea of an open, sunny spot very attractive for the winter months. A conservatory is not, however, a small investment, so it is important to plan carefully.

● Decide how your conservatory is to be used: will it be a family or breakfast room, or just used for growing plants?

● Positioning is vital – there's no point placing your 'sun room' on the dark side of the house. If you wish to produce a 'solar heating' effect within the room, ensure the sun-facing windows are large and double-glazed.

● Ideally, your conservatory will open directly from the interior of the house. If it's to be used as a living space, decorate as you would the rest of your home, bearing in mind that the sun will fade soft furnishings.

● Plan for the warm months as well as the cold: thermal blinds are perfect for ensuring your conservatory doesn't become a hothouse in summer! Deciduous trees will provide shade when it's needed, dropping their leaves to let in the winter sunshine. *This conservatory is the owner's winter room as it is in the sun for most of the day. Cedar windows and ceramic tiles help create an eclectic country look.*

CALLING IN THE EXPERTS

If garden and landscape design isn't your forte, it's easy to get help. Good garden design advice needn't cost the earth and can help you to avoid costly mistakes. Most designers will visit your house and offer an initial consultation at an hourly rate. Some will also provide plans so you can do the work yourself. Others will be happy to plan the job so that it can be completed in stages as your budget allows.

Before you call any landscape professional, work out the sort of help you need and how much you're willing to spend on the garden. Be realistic about what you can achieve for your budget. Most sites require some sort of construction work involving equipment, labour and materials, and this requires substantial amounts of money. People who design gardens can have varying qualifications, areas of expertise, rates and services offered. Be prepared to ask people about their qualifications, insurance, and to seek information about other work they've completed. Most importantly, make sure that they are willing to work happily with the budget you have in mind. Here are a few definitions to help you in making your decision:

Garden designers are experienced in plants and gardening, ideally with a qualification in horticulture. They can advise you about planting, maintaining and making the most of an existing garden. Unless they are a licensed builder, they may be unable to take on extensive construction work such as drainage, steps, paving and building walls. You will have to find your own contractors to undertake these tasks. Before selecting a gardener designer, ask a few about their horticultural qualifications and whether they are members of a professional body such as the Australian Institute of Horticulture.

Landscape contractors are the ones to call when you've got a garden that needs a lot of structural work. Landscape contractors move soil, sort out drainage issues, build walls and steps, lay paving and build structures such as pergolas and water features. Most landscape contractors will design, build and plant a garden. They are a good choice where a garden is to undergo a major renovation or if you are starting from scratch. Good landscape contractors will have tertiary training, a builder's licence and will be members of a professional landscaping association.

Landscape designers will have tertiary qualifications in landscape design and a sound knowledge of garden construction and of plants. All this comes at a price. A landscape designer will create a unique plan for your garden and then oversee the construction and planting. Most will be members of a professional landscape design association and will employ or recommend a construction team to carry out the work.

Landscape architects are the top of the garden design chain, with qualifications in landscape architecture from university. As you might expect, a landscape architect is the most expensive landscape design option. If you have a difficult site, an architect-designed or heritage house, and big plans for the garden, they may be your best choice. A landscape architect will design and oversee construction of the entire garden. If you are building a new home, try to get the landscape architect involved from the beginning. Most will be members of a professional landscape architecture association.

INDIAN ENCLOSURE

Essence: A formal style with structured plantings and wide paths, it traditionally featured a walled garden laid out in a geometric pattern, with water running along rills and the playing of fountains. Later, gardens followed an English pattern using tropical or monsoonal plants.

Architecture: Islamic patterns, walls with niches, pavilions with intricate stone carving and plants chosen for their fruit and their fragrance.

Features: A formal water feature with connecting canals or rills, orchards of fruit trees, containers of colourful plants.

Plants: A modern interpretation of an Indian garden might contain frangipani and gardenia, crepe myrtle and citrus trees, such as oranges and limes, with perhaps colourful beds of cannas and annuals. Shade trees were an important feature to cool the hot climate.

Colour: Bright colours in summer; pastels get lost in the heat so use bolder shades.

In a small suburban courtyard in Canberra, Hindu and Islamic traditions are married. A statue of a Hindu dancing girl stands at the far end of the courtyard above a carved marble water feature. A retaining wall was built to raise the end of the garden so the statue appears more prominent. Beneath, a small bubbling fountain is the central focus of a rectangular pool lined with decorative tiles. Water flows down a hand-carved chute into a smaller pool below. Typical Islamic influences of blue-black stones set into a pattern of arabesque scrolls dominate the courtyard. The result is a unique mosaic terrace, a peaceful place to relax, and an exquisite combination of imaginative design and a passion for India's Mogul gardens.

BRAZILIAN PATIO

Essence: Bold abstract forms, a painting on the ground, with plantings of grasses, foliage and texture plants used in broad sweeps and flowing lines. It is based on the work of Roberto Burle Marx, the famed Brazilian landscape architect.

Architecture: In its truest form, it harks back to ancient Amerindian designs with pyramid, monolithic masonry and carved walls, patterning with pebbles, stone and geometric shapes.

Features: Mosaics, bold colours, free-form shapes, landscape as art and solid masonry walls.

Plants: Mostly tropical in Brazil but plants can be adapted to suit the locality. Bold sweeps of plants with coloured leaves, like coleus, bromeliads, rhoeo and chlorophytum (spider plant), or common plants used uncommonly such as massed daylilies or scarlet salvias, punctuated by specimen architectural plants with bold foliage or form.

Colour: Earthy, hard landscaping colours with masses of green vegetation interspersed with blocks of coloured foliage.

Flamboyant artistry and exuberant creativity are the hallmarks of Brazil's famous garden designer, Roberto Burle Marx. The owners of this Canberra garden have paid homage to Marx's work, using a palette of purple, blue and white against a sea of green. A six-metre-long sculptural wall, patterned with mosaics, swoops up and down, at its feet sits a pond of water with pampas grass close by. White river pebbles and stepping stones take the visitor through the garden where walls are ivy-clad and alive with religious symbology.

1 2 3 4
5 6 7 8

LAWN ALTERNATIVES

Do you want something green but you don't want to mow it? There are some great lawn alternatives around, particularly for shaded or moist spots, such as under trees, where it is difficult to get lawn grasses to grow. But, a word of warning, most are not resilient enough to survive the wear and tear of a game of cricket.

Unlike normal grass lawns, these no-mow alternatives are not available in the form of ready-to-lay turf, so planting and establishing is a little more difficult than grass. Some, like the flat ground cover plant known as kidney weed or dichondra (*Dichondra micrantha*), can be grown from

seed, which is the ideal way to cover large areas. Others can be bought as small pots and divided into plugs or small sections for planting to cover a large area. From each plug, the plant will grow out to cover around 30cm or so (depending on the plant choice). Keep the area between the establishing plants weed free with weed mat, mulch or the use of a pre-emergent herbicide. Where a quick coverage is needed, you'll have to plant the plugs more closely. Mondo grass, which is widely used in landscaping, is often available nowadays by the metre, making it an economical choice for a large area.

1. Sandstone slabs make a pathway across a shaded area green with ivy and helxine.
2. Thyme is a lawn alternative for a hot, sunny spot. Well grown, it will even tolerate some light foot traffic. It has a wonderful fragrance, especially when crushed underfoot or brushed against.
3. Pebbles laid on edge give a garden a Mediterranean look. Here the smooth river stones are set in a sea of dichondra.
4. Mini mondo grass (*Ophiopogon japonicus* 'Nana') is used in this stylish setting to break up a flat area of paving. It is an excellent choice to edge or divide paving as it is only around 10cm tall.

5. Chamomile is a favoured lawn alternative in cooler areas. Here it is in full flower, but for those who prefer their lawns to stay green year round, seek out the form sold as 'Treneague', which rarely flowers.
6. Native violet (*Viola hederacea*) is one of the best of all lawn alternatives for a moist, shaded spot. As well as neat foliage, it also blooms with small violet flowers.
7. Helxine or baby's tears (*Soleirolia soleirolii*) is a soft creeping plant with tiny round leaves. It spreads forever when conditions are moist and shady but only reaches 5cm high.
8. Mondo grass is a tall, grassy alternative to normal lawns.

ORNAMENTAL GRASSES

Garden design has progressed in leaps and bounds over recent years. No longer are amateur gardeners restricting themselves to floral displays in their gardens; instead they're reaching into the entire plant design palette, particularly foliage texture and colour. For this reason, the use of ornamental grasses is on the rise. The strappy rustling fronds of Australian and New Zealand grasses are popping up in many forms: clumped together in rock gardens, massed in small, low-maintenance courtyards, used as edgings, or in garden borders. With leaf colours ranging from bronze through red, green, silver, yellow and blue-grey, they create striking backdrops for other plants, while some feature feathery or fluffy 'heads' (hare's tail grass, squirrel tail barley). Whether they are variegated, with stripes or cross-bandings, or in single shades of copper, green and tan, ornamental grasses can also look stunning grown in large urns or planted around a plinth.

1 *Spiky xanthorrhoea with blue forget-me-nots.* 2 Pennisetum orientale. 3 *Panicum.* 4 Miscanthus sinensis *'Zebrinus'.* 5 *Sedum, society garlic and miscanthus.* 6 Calamagrostis x acutiflora *'Karl Foerster'.* 7 *Mixed grasses including blue fescue.* 8 *Yellow fennel flowers with forget-me-nots and the fluffy seed heads of miscanthus.*

CLIMBERS

When training a climbing plant over a structure such as an arch or pergola, make the most of the size and space by selecting climbers that look good from below; add to the impact by planting those with fragrant flowers. Plant supports need to be strongly built as they have to carry the weight of a fully grown plant. When selecting a climbing plant, find out how it climbs. It may use tendrils (like clematis or grapevine), hooks, suction pads (such as ivy or Boston ivy) or the entire stem may wrap around the support. Some climbers, including the ever-popular roses, need to be tied to their support. Use a soft tie that doesn't cut into the growing branches. Plant ties, including grafting tape, are available from nurseries.

1. Banksia roses provide fast-growing cover for a pergola, fence or arch. They have the bonus of few thorns, evergreen growth in warm climates, and clusters of yellow or white flowers. The white-flowered form, *Rosa banksiae* 'Alba Plena', has a sweet perfume of violets and is thornless. Left unchecked, these roses can engulf their support, so keep them in shape by pruning after flowering in late spring or early summer.

2. Roses are a good choice for a sunny arch but need to be well trained. Select the colour and style that appeals. Shown here is the perfumed climber 'Pierre de Ronsard'.

3. Wisteria looks gorgeous draped over an arch or pergola. Its cascades of pendulous mauve, pink or white flowers are a breathtaking sight in spring and its perfume is overwhelming. It is a rampant climber that needs pruning from all angles to keep it in check. Prune after flowering in spring and summer. The flowers may be followed by long bean-like pods. Wisterias are deciduous climbers that lose their leaves in winter, so they are a good choice for summer shade and winter sun.
Other fragrant climbers include the chocolate vine (*Akebia quinata*), jasmines of all kinds, honeysuckle, the snail vine (*Vigna caracalla*), star jasmine (*Trachelospermum jasminoides*), stephanotis (*S. floribunda*), sweet peas (*Lathyrus odoratus*) and white mandevilla (*Mandevilla laxa*).

4. Clematis is one of the most beautiful flowering climbers for climates with cool summers. There are not only the large-flowered forms, such as 'Nelly Moser' shown here, but also the small-flowered forms, including native species. For success with clematis, keep the root area cool, shaded and moist, but allow the plant to climb into the sunlight. Feed in early spring and summer with potash-rich fertiliser.

5. Grapes were designed for pergolas. They are fast growing, colourful in autumn, and let the winter sun stream through. They are also very long lived but need to be kept in check by regular pruning and training. If you don't want the extra work involved in fruiting vines, select ornamental varieties.

WEED WARNING

Many once-popular water plants are now considered weeds. Avoid them in your pond as they could escape into natural watercourses.

Water hyacinth: gorgeous mauve flowers, easy to grow but banned in most waterways as it takes over.

Duck weed: covers the pond and clogs up filters.

Ferny azolla: pretty floating fern-like leaves, but it doubles every day and can cover the entire pond in a very short time. An excellent alternative is the native floating fern, nardoo.

Reeds and rushes: tall, elegant and easy to grow but will also take over. Keep in submerged pots. Don't plant in dams or around pond edges.

WATER PLANTS

Garden ponds and pools open up a new style of gardening and introduce a relaxing element. Floating waterlilies or tall exotic lotus can be part of your garden vision as can tall clumps of reeds, irises or bog plants. Which plants will grow and flower in a water garden is guided by two things. The first is the amount of sun (waterlilies, for example, prefer full sun) and the second is the depth of the water. Waterlilies will not grow in very shallow water (less than 30cm). In these areas use ornamental pebbles or surround the pond with plants that grow in boggy situations, such as papyrus or water iris. However, provided your pond is at least 30-50cm deep, you will be able to grow waterlilies successfully.

6. Thalia is a clump-forming water plant for the edges of ponds. It has violet-blue flowers during summer.

7. Papyrus can be grown in the ground beside a pond or grown in a pot and submerged into a pond. In a smaller area, select the dwarf papyrus, but where space isn't a problem enjoy the tall papyrus shown here.

8. Canna lilies come in a range of bold, bright colours, with orange, red or yellow flowers. Some varieties have boldly patterned or coloured leaves. They are ideal for shallow water or moist soil and flower in the warmer months of the year, then die back over winter.

9. Water irises bring height and colour to water gardens and have long-lasting summer flowers. These plants, such as the yellow-flowered *Iris pseudacorus*, are great used in clumps around the edge of a pond as they grow particularly well in boggy soil.

10. 'Green Goddess' is a green-flowered arum lily that can be grown in or beside water, or in any moist spot in the garden, in sun or shade.

11. Waterlilies are everyone's favourite water plant. They are available in a range of colours and flower sizes, with varieties to suit all climates. They are best grown in mesh baskets filled with a mix of soil and manure. Protect the soil surface with a mulch of gravel 2-5cm deep. Gradually submerge the pots into the water. Miniatures are more suited to small ponds but some will easily grow in around 90cm or more of water.

SCREENING

Evergreen shrubs with small leaves and growth that can be easily pruned and shaped are excellent privacy plantings. Before planting, check the ultimate height and spread of any shrub you are using as a hedge plant. Even if you intend to prune regularly, plants that grow far too big for their location will be a nightmare in time. Where possible, choose compact forms. To get the best from your screening hedge, begin trimming while plants are still young. Slightly taper the plants so they are narrower at the top to allow sunlight to reach the base of the plant. This encourages growth to the ground. If you are planning a geometric hedge, get into the habit of trimming it against a stringline to keep the lines of the hedge clean and straight.

1. *Syzygium* **'Elite'** and a row of pencil pines provide height while the golden duranta 'Sheena's Gold' forms a clipped border.
2. **Camellias** are excellent for screening as they are dense, evergreen and can be clipped.
3. **Ivy geranium** adds a bold colour contrast to the row of blue conifers shielding the pool.
4. **Box** makes a low screen that can be clipped into any shape.
5. **Conifers** are widely grown as screening plants as they are dense, evergreen and long lived.
6. **Sasanqua camellias** have been trained into a colourful evergreen hedge in a narrow area. Box adds a formal element.
7. **Teucrium** (*T. fruticans*) is used to form a privacy screen at the rear of this pool. It is a handsome shrub with aromatic, silver-grey leaves and blue spring flowers.

8 **9**

10 **11**

12

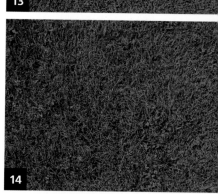

13

14

15

LAWNS

Lawns are really just green, high-maintenance garden floors. If you don't want to mow, trim the edges, water and fertilise, consider instead paving, concrete, pebbles, decking or the lawn alternatives on page 95. If you do want that smooth green sward, either for a play area or to offset the surrounding garden, select the grass that best suits your climate and matches your willingness to mow and trim. There are lawns for cool climates (known as cool-season grasses and including ryes, fescues and bent) and lawns for temperate to hot climates (warm-season grasses such as kikuyu, couch and buffalo). If grown in cooler areas, many warm-season grasses will lose their colour during winter.

8. Queensland blue couch is used in this subtropical garden. It is a quick-growing grass that does best in a warm to subtropical coastal climate. It will need regular and frequent mowing to keep it in check, especially through the warm, wet months of the year.

9. Lawn daisies may appear in cool-climate lawns, adding a meadow-like touch to the garden. The change in level here has resulted in a gentle slope that is still manageable by a hand lawnmower.

10. Buffalo is an excellent choice for a warm, coastal planting and some recent varieties, such as 'Sir Walter', 'Palmetto' and 'Shademaster', are softer to the touch and will tolerate light shade. It can be killed in frosty conditions.

11. Durban grass (also called sweet smother) grows in most areas but does very well in warm climates and in shaded spots. The key to success is to allow it to develop a long leaf blade. Here it is edged with mondo grass.

12. Kikuyu is an ideal choice for heavy traffic areas as it is vigorous and hard-wearing.

13. 'Windsorgreen' couch, along with 'Greenlees Park', suits the average backyard. Fine couches such as 'Santa Ana' are high-maintenance lawns.

14. Zoysia grass is becoming popular, particularly in tropical areas. It is low maintenance and, if well established, needs little watering.

15. Kentucky blue grass is a tough grass suited to cool gardens. This variety is 'Alpine'.

In this artist's garden (see also overleaf), lavender and roses provide a fragrant backdrop for a garden 'still life'. Plants can be used to create any effect you can imagine, provided you consider location and climate.

personal gardens

A garden is an individual work of art; the living expression of your personal view of the world. It can be serene and minimalist, a riot of colour and texture, or provide you with a harvest of fresh fruit and vegetables. You can incorporate painterly masterpieces, striking sculptures, or the embodiment of your spiritual beliefs. The beauty of working with nature is that there's no right and no wrong, only good and better. While passion may rule the heart of your design, don't forget the practical considerations that will give it life. Base your vision on grounded information, nurture it with care, and enjoy it through the seasons.

THE ARTIST'S GARDEN

*The personality of the artist
owner is seen in every detail
of this garden. Using colour,
texture, light and shade, she
has created painterly 'pictures'
at every turn. Decoration
takes the form of statuary
surrounded by a sea of African
daisies (above) to provide
a shock of colour, or rustic
still-life compositions (left and
opposite below), which take
their inspiration from the rural
environment. While seemingly
artless in appearance, a
painterly garden takes careful
planning, and consideration
must be given to seasonality
and foliage texture. Colours
are either strongly contrasting,
such as in the lavender and
photinia (opposite above), or
blended to create a seamless
vista to the hills beyond.*

In the artist's garden, a treillage is draped with purple wisteria for spring flowers, summer shade and winter sun.

nurturing your garden

The care that you lavish on your garden will be rewarded as you watch it flourish. However, it will demand your attention throughout the year. Regardless of the season, there are always tasks to perform to keep your garden looking at its best.

SPRING
PLANTING

Preparation is a key factor in successful planting. Clear away grass and weeds, removing underground roots and runners as well as the leafy top growth. Then dig in lots of compost, well-rotted manure or a load of organic soil conditioner.

PRUNING

Early in the season, prune away any wind- or frost-damaged parts of plants. Cut back damaged growth to healthy wood. New shoots will develop quickly.

Later, as plants finish their early rush of flowers, lightly prune ('dead head') to remove any spent flowers. Often a second floral flush will follow as a result.

Dead head: spring-flowering roses (eg, banksia roses), spring bulbs (remove spent flowers but leave foliage to die back naturally), bottlebrush, blossom trees, daisies, azaleas and rhododendrons.

● Spring is also the time to shape plants so they become more compact. Any new growth can be tip pruned (also called pinch pruned) for a bushy look. Simply pinch out the new growth tip to encourage two tips to form in its place.

Tip prune: annuals such as petunias, along with fuchsias and evergreen hedges.

WATERING

Deep water new plants, pots and any shrubs. As the temperature starts to rise, especially overnight, you will see some activity with the lawns, too – get the sprinkler out to give everything in the garden a good soaking.

Check the watering system: If you've got a watering system but haven't used it much over winter, give it a thorough check and clean. Clean out the inline filter and then turn on the taps. Walk around the system's route, checking for dislodged sprinklers or blockages and then repair and clean where necessary.

FEEDING

If you don't remember anything else, remember this: give every plant in your garden some plant food in spring. Buy a big bag of Dynamic Lifter, or some tubs of slow-release plant food, and scatter it everywhere. Once you've tossed the food around, water it well into the soil (fertilising just after rain is also a good idea). Pay particular attention to the feeding of hibiscus, roses and citrus.

Small areas: Even the smallest pot plants will appreciate some food now – you can liquid feed these using a soluble fertiliser and a watering can.

Lawns: Invest in a complete, slow-release lawn food. Scatter it all over your lawn >

HERB GARDEN

A herb garden may sound like a romantic notion, but it is actually one of the most practical ideas in gardening. Herbs add enormous flavour to cooking and can be used for all kinds of medicinal purposes, yet they don't require a lot of space and can be grown in pots for ready access. In fact, the only thing you need in abundance for a herb garden is sunlight. You can create an interesting effect by using different-sized pots, perhaps all in terracotta which looks great and drains well. A large, round, shallow pot is ideal for fast-growing herbs such as parsley and basil. Or try a planter box – you can buy pots of advanced herbs which you simply insert into the box, or fill the box with potting mix and plant your herbs in a row. If you're planning a permanent garden, say in a bed or a half wine barrel, think of the design of your plantings. Some herbs are as decorative as they are useful – parsley and chives make good border plantings, while prostrate thyme can be used to trail over a planter box or pot. Common sage (*Salvia officinalis*), with its grey-green leaves, looks particularly effective as an underplanting for a larger plant in a terracotta pot.

THE SCULPTOR'S GARDEN

Generally, the rule for using statuary in the garden is that old favourite: less is more. But this creative and unusual space in Oatlands, Tasmania, goes a long way to disproving the rule. Designed around the weathered timber buildings and stonework of a 19th-century farmyard, the garden features starkly beautiful sculptures made from discarded farm machinery. Soft cottage-style plantings blend with the stronger lines of natives to provide a natural setting for the man-made pieces. A water feature provides a meeting place for the two elements. When using sculpture in your garden, take inspiration from the environment and consider the overall 'theme' that you want to achieve in your space.

< following the directions on the pack. For large areas, use a fertiliser spreader to make sure the food is evenly distributed. If you decide to use a hose-end applicator and a weed-and-feed product, read the instructions carefully before you start. It may not suit all lawn types.

WEEDING

Doing a little bit of weeding and tidying each day in spring will help to keep weeds under control. Hand weed with a trowel, use a hoe or spray with a herbicide such as glyphosate (keeping it well away from any plant you want to keep), to maintain the garden in a weed-free state.

Replenish mulch: Organic mulch around the garden will have broken down over winter. Order in a load of good-quality organic garden mulch (such as lucerne, sugar cane or composted pinebark) and spread it throughout the garden. For a bit of extra-quick feeding, you can mix in some well-rotted manure.

PLANNING AHEAD

Now's the time to take stock of your garden and make plans for next year. Visit your local nursery and buy plants in flower for a good instant show and for future years too. Also look at what should be planted now to keep the garden interesting in the months ahead. Punnets of annuals, summer-flowering bulb packs, waterlilies and even seed packets all contain the flowers you'll want in bloom in summer. Buy and plant now!

Vegetable planting plan: Plant tomatoes, capsicum, cucumbers, zucchini, melons and pumpkins.

Flower planting plan: Plant marigolds, dahlias, cosmos, snapdragons, nasturtiums and Californian poppies.

SEASONAL TIPS

Don't get complacent. Spring can be a very finicky time of the year. Hot, windy days followed by sudden cold spells with late frosts are all to be expected during this season. Be aware that late frosts can damage spring flower buds, tender new growth and new plantings.

Take care: Particularly if you live in a southern or inland spot, be cautious with new plants and remember to cover overnight anything that's frost-prone (such as tomatoes), just to be on the safe side. Don't forget to remove the cover during the day. Frost is most likely to occur when nights are clear and still. >

THE COLLECTIVE GARDEN

Permaculture principles are the underlying philosophy of this vital community garden in Sydney. Run by the University of NSW since 1993, the garden emphasises reuse, recycling and reduction of waste. Permaculture is the production of food using multi-purpose plants (those which are food for both humans and animals) and animals that recycle nutrients and keep down weeds (usually chickens). Students and local volunteers work daily in this garden, creating a bounty of edible produce (see pomegranate, below, and 'Queensland Blue' pumpkin, below right). Community garden groups nurture an interest in organic farming, as many espouse such principles.

< SUMMER

PLANTING

Summer is a great time to put in new plants, provided you'll be around to keep them well watered. If you're planning to head off on holidays, put planting plans on hold until you return.

Water what you plant: Treat any new plantings as if they are still in a pot. Their root systems will not be well enough established to support water loss, especially on hot days. If you notice that they are becoming very wilted, increase watering and provide them with shade until they become more established.

PRUNING

Summer pruning is all about gaining control of your garden. Keep wayward climbing and creeping plants in check by both pruning and training them.

Prune to control: Wisterias and other rampant climbing plants can be pruned as necessary over summer.

● Lightly clip hedges and remove spent flower heads in late summer. Cut back anything that's past its best.

Dead heading and tidying: Agapanthus, fuchsias, hydrangeas, weigela, gaura, annuals and summer-flowering perennials can all be tidied up.

● Roses will need a light pruning in late summer to promote further flowering.

Rose prune: This isn't the hard prune of winter, but simply a light cutting back to remove spent flower stems and to encourage an autumn flush of flowers in six to eight weeks' time.

>

< WATERING

Watering is a priority over long hot summers. Concentrate on giving the entire garden (including the lawn) a deep, thorough watering once or twice a week. Water new plantings, pot plants, annuals and vegies daily. If plants are wilting, water them immediately.

Morning or afternoon: Is it better to water gardens in the morning or in the evening? The key is to suit yourself (and heed any restrictions that may be in place). If you water in the morning you set the garden up to survive a hot day. Watering later will revive the garden but could lead to fungal problems around vulnerable plants that stay wet overnight.

It's not just the garden that needs water. Most water features, particularly those that splash or trickle, lose a lot of water through evaporation. Top up the reservoir of water frequently so your pump does not burn out.

FEEDING

Plants that are growing at a pace will appreciate extra food in the summer months. A good way to keep the nourishment in the soil is to add compost or manure to the existing layer of mulch.

Vegetables: The leafy vegetables that we all enjoy eating over summer, such as Asian greens and soft-hearted lettuce, need to be kept growing quickly. You can achieve this with fortnightly liquid feeding and daily watering.

Summer feeding: Plants that are going to keep growing and flowering through summer and into autumn will benefit from extra food. Summer-feed roses, >

HOME OFFICE GARDEN

This home office, under a Brisbane house, takes full advantage of its proximity to the pool and garden. Here, work and play areas converge, while maintaining distinct identities and roles. Potted conifers supply a visual link between the interior surfaces of concrete-and-chrome and the greenery outdoors. The low-maintenance plantings of philodendrons and wisteria ensure that the owner, an architect, is not confronted daily by garden chores, yet they still provide a congenial atmosphere for outdoor client meetings. When planning a garden to complement a home office, ensure adequate lighting and clear pathways for the safety of your clients.

LOOKING AFTER YOURSELF IN THE GARDEN

Gardening brings with it some safety considerations:
● Choose the right clothing. Closed shoes are necessary, particularly when using machinery or sharp, heavy tools. Wear a long-sleeved cotton shirt to protect against thorns and prickles, and, of course, the sun. A broad-brimmed hat is essential, as is sunscreen.
● If you're using a hedge trimmer, mower or similar appliance, wear goggles to protect against flying debris.
● Technique is important in digging: drive the blade into the soil, then pull down on the handle to lift the soil, keeping your back straight and bending your knees for leverage. It's important not to bend your back when digging, lifting or forking – always bend at the knees.
● Switch off and unplug electrical machines when not in use, and prior to cleaning and maintenance.
● Keep the blades of garden tools sheathed in plastic or leather covers when not in use. Don't put secateurs in your pocket between jobs.
● Always wear gloves when pruning, weeding and handling potting mixtures.
● Potting mix and compost contain micro-organisms that can be harmful. Avoid inhaling dust from either.
● Ensure that your tetanus boosters are up to date.

BALINESE GARDEN

A love of all things Balinese was the inspiration for this oasis in inner-city Sydney. Based on a series of platforms, the garden features a pergola (left), with nasturtiums and clerodendrums. Plantings have been chosen for exuberant foliage (assorted ferns and bamboos), fragrance (buddleia, frangipani) and colour (bougainvillea, agapanthus). The finishing touch is a custom-made flag, based on those used in Bali during festivals. The key to re-creating a tropical-style garden at home is to use plants that evoke the mood you are after (for example, large leaves, bright colours), but that work in your own backyard. Authentic touches – statuary, painted walls, textures – will contribute greatly to the overall effect.

< citrus, hibiscus, camellias and all lawns (water them well after applying food).

WEEDING

Sometimes in summer you might feel that there are more weeds than plants – for successful removal, clear small areas at a time. Remember that most weeds readily regrow either from underground pieces (such as bulbs, stems and roots) or from small pieces of top growth (such as the fleshy stems of wandering jew). Many also produce seed heads. Ensure that removed weeds are carefully bagged up and thrown into the garbage, rather than added to the compost bin.

Replenish mulch again: Good mulch breaks down and feeds the soil. As this happens, top it up with more on the surface. Mulch keeps the soil cool, suppresses weeds and stops moisture loss.

PLANNING AHEAD

Late summer is the time to plan ahead for autumn, winter and spring. Bulbs appear in nurseries, as do winter annuals. Clear away all those spent annuals and perennials to make way for fresh new growth.

Vegetable planting plan: Plant late tomatoes, capsicum, eggplant (in warm zones), beans, herbs, beetroot, cucumber, lettuce.

Flower planting plan: Plant primulas, pansies, poppies and sweet peas in late summer months.

SEASONAL TIPS

If you've spent all summer sweating, think about planting some shade. A deciduous tree that is planted on the north or north-western side of your house will act as an external air-conditioner. Or invest in a pergola and add a fast-growing climber, such as an ornamental grapevine.   >

< AUTUMN

PLANTING

Autumn is one of the best seasons for planting, as plants have time to get their roots established before winter.

Choosing good plants: By the end of summer, plants that have been in pots for many months have outgrown the potting mix and even the pot. If a plant is wilting even though it is being watered, blows over readily or has a thick mat of roots when you remove it from its pot, it is pot-bound. Severely pot-bound plants often fail to grow when they're planted out, so avoid buying them from the nursery. If your own plants are looking pot bound, repot them into a slightly larger pot with fresh potting mix. Lightly prune away any congested or knotted roots and treat with a seaweed-based plant conditioner.

Bulb planting: Spring-flowering bulbs must all be planted before the end of autumn. Tulips benefit from a six-week spell in the crisper section of your fridge before they're planted. Buy them in March, chill them and then plant in early May. As a rule of thumb, plant spring-flowering bulbs at twice their width.

PRUNING

While autumn isn't the time to massively prune, it is the time to do that annual clean-up. Rip out all that tired summer growth to revitalise your entire garden. Give hedges a final clip in early autumn.

Don't prune: While it's good to tidy up most plants, avoid pruning frost-sensitive plants and any tropical or subtropical plants if you have a cool winter. Prune these plants in early spring.

A COOK'S GARDEN

As our interest in fresh food continues to grow, so too does the popularity of the productive garden. This potager (opposite) is in the NSW Southern Highlands. Built from local sandstone, it is the perfect cook's garden – raised beds allow for easy picking and maintenance, wide paths for access, and the circular shape ensures part of the garden is always in the sun. Herbs are planted in the middle section and seasonal vegetables (such as silverbeet, left, and beans climbing up willow, above) in surrounding beds, interplanted with nasturtiums and marigolds to keep pests at bay. A fine mulch of eucalyptus leaves keeps weeds under control and moisture in; it also deters snails.

WATERING

Watering can be reduced but be prepared for sudden blistering heat at any time. Keep watering vegetables and annuals.

Run-off: If you notice that water is simply running off the surface, leaving the soil beneath bone dry, you need to add a soil conditioner or surfactant to your watering. This chemical helps change the structure of the soil's surface so water soaks in. Sandy soils are particularly vulnerable as are soils that have been compacted through summer. Follow up by improving the soil with organic matter.

FEEDING

Plants that are winding down as the weather cools don't need to be fed. Plants that are still growing and flowering in autumn will need to be fed.

What to feed in autumn: Productive vegetables, new annuals and plants that grow and flower through autumn and winter.

WEEDING

If using a herbicide to kill off weed growth, it will take longer to be effective as the weather cools and growth slows.

Persistent lawn weeds: If you were irritated by prickles in your lawn through summer, plan to treat the new growth in late autumn or early winter. Top of the list is bindii, which can be removed by a selective herbicide and by improving soil compaction through aeration.

PLANNING AHEAD

The forward planning continues in autumn. Plant winter vegetables and spring-flowering shrubs and trees now.

Vegetable planting plan: Plant the brassicas (broccoli, cabbage, cauliflower), along with broad beans, asparagus and rhubarb crowns, onions, garlic, winter lettuce.
Flower planting plan: Plant primulas, pansies, spring bulbs and sweet peas.

SEASONAL TIPS

Make the most of the autumn leaf bonanza by collecting fallen leaves and adding them to your compost heap. Leaf mulch breaks down into one of the best natural plant foods you can make at home, so don't let it go to waste.

Making compost: The quickest way to deal with fallen leaves is just to heap them onto the garden as instant mulch. Alternatively, bag them up in large garbage bags and leave them out of the way to break down slowly until spring.   >

117

A COLLECTOR'S GARDEN

The owner of this Sydney garden concedes that it's overplanted but, as a proud 'plantsperson', she wouldn't have it any other way. Designed to offer seasonal interest, the garden (photographed here in summer) is planted around and under a framework of golden robinia trees. The east-facing garden is home to a variety of shade-loving plants, such as variegated chlorophytum, clivia, bromeliads and, notably, hydrangeas. Smaller plantings are changed regularly as the owner experiments with colour schemes. The backdrop of mature shrubs, however, ensures that the garden never looks bare while new plants are being established.

< WINTER

PLANTING

Plants that are dormant during winter, particularly the deciduous plants, love to be planted at this time. Roses, vines, fruit trees, deciduous trees and herbaceous perennials can all be planted in winter. Also readily available in winter are all the citrus trees, which will bear fruit through the winter months.

They're not just sticks: Although your deciduous plants may look like a bunch of sticks at this time of year, they will grow and expand rapidly once spring arrives. Take careful note of the expected size of anything that you plant when it's dormant and leave lots of space for it to grow and develop properly. This will reduce the amount of pruning and training that you'll have to do during the spring and summer months.

PRUNING

Plants that are bare in winter can also be pruned at this time of year. Top of the list for mid-to-late winter pruning are roses, but grapevines, hydrangeas and fruit trees will also benefit from judicious pruning.

Tree care: When deciduous trees are bare and leafless, take some time to check them over for damaged branches, signs of borer, or invasion by climbing plants, such as ivy, which can cause damage to the tree or harbour pests.

WATERING

Watering is a low priority in winter, although, of course, it should not be >

< forgotten altogether. Most plants need less frequent watering but all will benefit from a good deep drink after a bout of cold, dry winds. Pay particular attention to plants that are growing or flowering through winter. Keeping those plants well watered will mean a longer lasting flower display and better growth.

Camellias: These wonderful shrubs come into their own during winter but so often are neglected by gardeners. Brown flowers probably indicate lack of water so get out the hose and deep water camellias for longer flowering.

FEEDING

Keep the plant foods carefully stored during winter. Plants don't need to be fed when they're not growing. Winter vegetables and annuals, however, will appreciate a fortnightly liquid feed to keep them growing well.

Compost care: To keep the compost working well over winter, turn it from time to time. If the weather is very wet, you'll need to cover the compost heap to protect it from waterlogging in the rain.

WEEDING

Winter grass is a tufty bright green grass that invades lawns from autumn to spring. It will die out naturally as the weather warms. It can be killed with regular applications of a selective herbicide or simply leave it – small birds often depend on its seeds for winter feed.

Winter weeds: While most weeds graciously lie low over winter, a few come into their own. Seasonal trouble-makers include soursob (*Oxalis pes-caprae*) and fireweed, a small tufty plant with tiny, yellow, daisy-like flowers. It's best to avoid digging up soursob as its bulbs are deep in the soil and it will be easily spread through weeding. Treat it instead with herbicide. Fireweed and other winter weeds should be removed before they have the time to set seed.

PLANNING AHEAD

Good gardeners continue to look ahead, even in winter. As well as planting all deciduous trees, shrubs and climbers now, you should also start planting any annuals and perennials for flowers in spring and early summer.

Vegetable planting plan: Plant broad beans, artichokes, asparagus, silverbeet, onions, spring onions and peas.

Flower planting plan: Seeds of spring-flowering annuals, such as marigolds, petunias, cosmos and cleome, can be sown in seed trays (but don't plant them out until the soil warms). Plant seedlings at the end of winter.

SEASONAL TIPS

Divide and conquer – that's the rule of gardening in winter. Dormant plants, such as herbaceous perennials, or clumps of evergreen perennials, such as agapanthus and mondo grass, can be dug up, split into small clumps and replanted or potted to give away. It's also the time to take hardwood cuttings from deciduous plants. Late winter is also the best time of the year to renovate the garden by moving trees and shrubs to new locations.

Moving stories: Except for native plants, most of which resent being moved at any time, winter is the best time to dig up and move plants that are growing in the wrong spot. Dig around the root ball out at the dripline (that's at the edge of the leafy growth) and have some helpers on hand to manoeuvre anything that's large. Even a plant that's only a metre or so tall will have a heavy root ball. Prepare the plant's new home in advance so it can be dug up and replanted quickly.

PERSONAL SANCTUARY
Here was a space never used. The back garden, co-joining the downstairs living area, was just used as a thoroughfare. The new owners wanted to create a space where friends and family would 'stop and smell the roses'. Sydney garden designer Peter Nixon used just three varieties of plants to create a lush, dark-green backdrop for this family haven: mini mondo grass (Ophiopogon japonicus 'Nana'), lilly pilly (Syzygium australe 'Elite') and giant turf lily (Liriope muscari 'Evergreen Giant'). A statuesque sandstone sculpture by Chris Bennetts of Ishi Buki serves as the central focus in an area otherwise dominated by the pool. Concentric circles of white pebbles spread out from the statue in a reflection of the ripples that play across the water's surface. Simplicity is important when creating a serene effect – this is not the place for a riot of colour, rather the understated appeal of distinct textures.

VEGETABLES

The best vegies to grow are the ones that you and yours enjoy eating. Don't waste energy on vegies no one fancies. Of all the vegies, salad crops are the easiest and fastest to grow. Lettuce and most of the Asian greens, such as bok choy and senposai, can be planted just about year round. The soft-hearted lettuce varieties, such as 'Buttercrunch' or 'Red Coral', are a fast and tasty crop that can be squeezed in just about anywhere. Add to your home-grown salad with cucumbers and radishes. Also good to grow, colourful in the garden and delicious to eat are capsicum, chillies and tomatoes. The small cherry tomatoes are the easiest to grow of all the tomato varieties and range from tiny to bite-sized.

Over the years, home gardeners have decided that growing their own vegies is too much like hard work. There seems to be too many rules. Our advice is don't worry about the rules: vegies are fun to grow and very rewarding. Take the plunge and grow a crop somewhere in your garden, whether it's a potato plant or a pumpkin vine that grew by itself in the compost heap, or some lettuce seedlings you bought, on the spur of the moment, at your local nursery. Try a tomato seedling – plant it after winter has passed and you'll be picking succulent fruit in summer. Most vegies just need regular water, full sun and a quick check for obvious pest problems. Once you develop a taste for home-grown produce, you could be hooked!

1. Silverbeet can look stunning in the garden and will be productive in most areas all year round. Its large, thick leaves add colour and drama to the vegie patch. In warm climates it is easier to grow than English spinach. This red stemmed variety is sweet and fast growing.

2. Carrots are delicious to eat pulled fresh from the earth. To ensure straight carrots, prepare the ground before planting by digging over to remove any lumps or stones. If the carrot hits a hard spot in the soil it may fork or become distorted. A free-draining sandy loam is ideal. In most areas, carrots can be sown all year round.

3. Snow peas are a tasty and fast-growing crop. Harvest them young and tender. Train them onto a trellis or, if space is tight, a simple tripod made from garden canes. There are also dwarf snow pea varieties.

4. Red geraniums mixed in with the crops make your vegie patch look good. Other colourful companion plants include French marigolds, calendulas, pansies and dwarf nasturtiums. For foliage colour, use blocks of leafy vegies, such as lettuce, kale (a show stopper in autumn) or Asian greens.

5. Lettuce leaves can be picked as needed, rather than uprooting the whole plant. And there's room for a little whimsy in even the most productive of garden areas. While the rabbit shown here is purely ornamental, where rabbits are a problem, you'll need to erect a rabbit-proof fence.

6. Artichokes, pictured here with leeks and carrots, are easy to grow and so handsome that they can even be featured in the garden border. They are grown from suckers planted between autumn and spring. Once established, plants grow and produce for many years.

7. Dwarf vegies may not need staking, but most vegies do. Tripods (seen here, centre right) can be made from several stakes tied together and used to support peas and beans.

8. Salad leaves make an attractive display in a sunny spot tucked in among flowers.

9. Tomatoes are popular because they're so easy to grow and taste delicious. Pictured here is a yellow cherry tomato, just one of the many unusual varieties available.

HERBS

Herbs are handy to have growing near the kitchen. Thai and Asian herbs add a wonderful zing to dishes, so consider growing lemon grass, Vietnamese mint, coriander and even ginger. Top choices to include in any herb garden are rocket, basil, chives, mint and parsley. Herbs need full sun and well-drained soil. The exception to this overall rule is mint, which tolerates some shade and enjoys moist soil. Most herbs grow throughout the warmer months of the year, dying down over winter. Some, like thyme and mint, last for many years, while others, such as basil, coriander and parsley, are replanted regularly as the quality of the leaf is lost when the plants begin to flower and form seed.

1. Chamomile is a herb that's enjoyed as a tea. It is low growing with ferny leaves and can form a lovely ground cover. In cool to mild climates with low humidity it can be used as an alternative to a lawn. In summer it produces a mass of small, daisy-like flowers and it is these flowers that are mainly infused in teas or for cosmetic use (it's a great hair rinse).

2. Fennel produces airy heads of flowers and, in autumn, seeds. This tall-growing herb has an anise flavour and can be enjoyed for its thick root or you can pick some leaves to flavour fish dishes and salads. It can become weedy as it self-seeds.

3. Mustards can be grown quickly and easily from seed. Eat the peppery leaves or enjoy the yellow flowers. This curly leafed mustard is well on its way to seeding.

4. Chives are among the easiest herbs to grow. The onion chives shown here have purple flowers and tubular leaves. Garlic chives have flat leaves and white flowers. Both forms enjoy a sunny spot and can be grown from seed, seedling or by dividing an existing clump.

5. Rosemary is aromatic all year round and in late summer and early autumn has a display of white or blue flowers. It can be grown as a ground cover or shrub and, if regularly clipped, can be used as a dense hedge.

6. The herb garden can become a feature by adding a sundial and a rustic brick path.

7. Curry plant, with its silver leaves, looks good in the garden and smells great, too. It can be added to chicken for flavour and the yellow flowers can be dried to add to homemade potpourri.

8. Chervil is a fast and easy herb to grow from seed. It's a great cut-and-come-again herb for semi-shade. Once it flowers, sow more seeds for fresh leaves.

9. Borage, with its decorative blue or white flowers, is sure to attract bees to your garden. Use the leaves when they're young to add a cucumber-like flavour to salads and sandwiches.

10. Pineapple sage has a lovely pineapple scent. Make the most of this by planting it in an area of the garden where it will be brushed to release its aroma. The red flower spires are highly attractive to small nectar-eating birds.

YEAR-ROUND SCENT

Plant
Season

Arabian jasmine (*Jasminum sambac* 'Grand Duke of Tuscany')
spring-autumn
Choisya (*C. ternata*)
spring-summer
Daphne (*D. odora*)
winter
Gardenia (*G. augusta* 'Florida')
summer
Lavender (many species and hybrids)
spring-summer
Murraya (*M. paniculata*)
summer-autumn
Osmanthus (*O. fragrans*)
winter-spring
Peppermint geranium (*Pelargonium tomentosum*)
all year (foliage)
Roses (select fragrant varieties)
spring-autumn
Viburnum (*V. odoratissimum*)
summer

8 9

FRAGRANT PLANTS

Add to your garden sanctuary with the gentle aromas from scented plants. Plant perfumes can be heady and overwhelming or soft and elusive. Sometimes plants are more perfumed by day, but some flowers have fragrance only at night. Select those that flower at different times for year-round fragrance. As a bonus, look for plants with fragrant foliage, such as scented geraniums, lavender and many herbs, including sage, rue and curry plant. Flowering favourites to provide fragrance at different times throughout the year include brown boronia, freesia, hyacinth, lily of the valley, mint bush, stephanotis, wisteria, tuberose and violets.

1. Mint bush (centre), like many Australian natives, is perfumed. It has attractive blue flowers but the scent is strongest from the leaves, particularly after rain or if they are brushed as you walk past them through the garden.

2. Star jasmine growing up a pergola near the house allows you to enjoy its scent each time you pass. Even in a small space, this wonderfully fragrant plant can be included as a clipped feature trained on lattice or wires. Peak flowering is in spring, but there will be the occasional flower at other times of the year too.

3. Scented shrubs and herbs make this garden fragrant year round from both flowers and aromatic foliage.

4. Gardenias are just about everyone's favourite fragrant flower. These small, evergreen shrubs bloom from spring to autumn but are best in a warm, humid climate. This flower is the florist's gardenia (*Gardenia augusta* 'Florida'), which forms a compact plant around a metre high. For a larger flower and larger shrub, seek out 'Magnifica', which can also be trained into a standard.

5. Lilac is a shrub that's easy to grow in cool-climate gardens. Enjoy its wonderfully scented flowers in spring.

6. Rose-scented geranium, with its fragrant foliage, can be relied on for year-round fragrance, especially as you brush by as it spreads over the garden steps, as seen here.

7. Lavender is a wonderfully fragrant plant, seen here in spring on a roof garden. It is happiest in full sun.

8. Roses come in all shapes and sizes, from low ground covers to vigorous climbers. Among the most fragrant are David Austin roses, which combine the scent of old roses with the repeat-flowering qualities of modern roses. Here a row of the long-flowering 'Bonica' is used as an informal hedge. Opposite the roses, erigeron daisies soften the stone edging.

9. Wallflowers will bring a delicious sweet fragrance to gardens in winter and spring, and will grow in most areas. Don't worry if you don't have a wall, they grow happily in the garden or even in a pot.

A paved eating area, tucked behind the stone walls of a beachfront Adelaide house, is sheltered from the gusty winds that are part of living close to the ocean. The owners replaced all the garden soil to ensure plants such as Salvia guaranitica and 'Iceberg' roses would thrive in their coastal environs.

small gardens

secrets

Whether it's a corner of a larger garden or the sum of the whole, even the smallest space can blossom. Plant a striking sculptural succulent in an earthy container to create a miniature green space. Bring a balcony to life with refreshing touches of foliage for a leafy perspective on life. Deck windows with bright splashes of fragrant colour in character-filled boxes. Or create a peaceful Oriental corner within a rambling acreage – or even a functional suburban block. While space may be limited, imagination is not and you can play with shape and scale to great effect. Be warned, however: little gardens require large amounts of planning.

planning a small garden

There are several basic considerations when you set about planning your small garden. One of the greatest problems you'll face is that of access. If your small space is upstairs, through the house, or down a narrow alleyway, moving large objects into the garden is always going to be tricky. Definitely weigh up the pros and cons first. If access is difficult, keep these constraints in mind when you decide what you want in your garden. Break things down into manageable amounts, such as bags of potting mix that you can lift, and lightweight containers.

Think creatively in your small space: the three simple guidelines you should follow are make the space work for you,

don't clutter the space, and choose plants that definitely will perform.

MAKING IT WORK

The first step, as with any garden, is site- and self-analysis. How do you want to use this small space? Is it an outdoor room to extend your living space? Is it a garden to look out upon from inside, like a picture on the wall? Is it the answer to your dream of self-sufficiency?

If it is a narrow walkway, for example, it may need to look (or smell) nice as you walk by but be easy to maintain.

Once you've come to terms with what you want, it'll be much easier to develop the space into a garden that works. If it is >

PAVED AREAS

Even the smallest room can be extended when opened up to the garden (above). And it doesn't matter what size your garden is, so long as there's space for sitting, dining and relaxing. Here, the landscape designer has created a sheltered spot for entertaining by laying pale grey paving stones. In this Melbourne courtyard (opposite), bone-coloured pavers laid in a 'stretcher' pattern and rendered walls visually expand the space. A row of slender Korean mountain ash trees draws the eye to a dark nib wall. Their small root system makes these trees ideal for small gardens.

WALLED SPACES

If your garden is protected by high walls, paint them to provide a link with the indoors. When the doors of this Melbourne house (opposite) are open, the living space spills into the paved courtyard garden with its smart chequered tile plunge pool and exotic furniture from the Philippines, made from bamboo and recycled tyres. By planting the perimeter of the courtyard, an open oasis of space is achieved. This compact roof garden (right), part of a converted warehouse in Adelaide, was given a high brick wall for privacy. The slate-topped garden bed against the wall incorporates bench seating plus a fountain and fish pond, with a carved timber screen mounted on the wall above. In keeping with the building's industrial origins, the courtyard floor is plain concrete. A shade sail protects against the harsh sun by day, retracting at night for dinner under the stars.

< an outdoor living space, plan the garden around a table and chairs or somewhere comfortable to sit.

If it's to be a garden picture, plan and arrange the garden by looking at it very carefully from indoors.

If you're dreaming of self-sufficiency, find a sunny spot and start a herb patch or pot. You can also make the most of a narrow space with vertical plants, such as angel wing begonias.

MAKING THE MOST OF SPACE

One sure way to make a space seem small is to clutter it up with too many different things. Lots of differently sized, shaped and coloured pots are the usual culprits, closely followed by as many different wall colours and finishes as there are walls.

Be rigorous when planning a container garden. If you've acquired lots of small, impractical pots, repot their contents into larger pots, treating each large container as a mini garden. If a plant doesn't look good, or doesn't fit, find it a new home or redirect it to the compost heap.

If the existing pots are the right size but all look different, consider painting them to match or to tone together. Then arrange them in groups or patterns to make the most of your garden space.

If all the boundaries, that is the walls or fences in your garden, are different, introduce some unity here as well. You can make them whatever colour, texture or material you like. A coat of paint or lime wash is the quickest and easiest way to unify the boundaries of a small space.

Clever paint choices can be either made a feature or made to fade into the >

< background. Try colouring the walls to match your house, or even painting them blue to blend with the sky and so disappear into the background. To turn a wall from an eyesore into a feature, highlight it by painting it in a contrasting colour to the rest of the surroundings.

Walls that differ in appearance can also be clad, masked or disguised so that they all look the same. Lattice is the great garden disguiser. It can be cut into many shapes and sizes and used to make screens, arches and walls, or to block out untidy spots such as the area under the house. Lattice is also decorative, either in a building or as small panels like pictures, mounted on a wall.

Boundaries can also be covered with climbing plants, such as star jasmine, roses or mandevilla, transforming walls into vertical gardens, or use the wall as a place for a garden ornament. Wall fountains, mosaics or simple terracotta panels can turn a courtyard wall into a feature. Remember, if it is suspended on a wall, it isn't taking up valuable floor space.

PLANTS IN SMALL SPACES

Plants and their containers are the decorative elements in a small garden, much as cushions, rugs and ornaments are inside your house. If you can stop thinking of plants as vegetation and flowers, and think of them instead in terms of >

COURTYARDS

Order can be achieved from within a rambling garden (above) by using plants as courtyard 'walls' to give privacy and protection. These beautiful established trees make a delightfully lush boundary to the saltwater swimming pool and alfresco eating area of The Orangerie, a renowned guesthouse in Stirling, SA. The hard landscaping defines this Mediterranean-style outdoor living space (opposite). The designer has blurred the boundary by deliberately choosing the same flooring – concrete tiles bordered by darker pebbles – to make the transition from inside to out.

ROOFTOP GARDENS

City dwellers have created a retreat on a rooftop boardwalk, with wisteria planted to screen a neighbouring rendered wall (opposite). Pots and urns of flowering petunias love the sunny position and make a great show of colour.

Limit the plant varieties as these owners have done (above) and simply create a fringe of greenery around the perimeter. Big terracotta pots containing citrus trees or large flowering shrubs are ideal, but you'll need to plan the space to decide on the position of the containers. You won't want to move pots this heavy too often.

< colours, shapes and textures, you'll find it a lot easier to use them successfully in a small space. Don't start with a particular plant in your mind, begin instead with the look or the role you want that plant to perform.

Of course, in order for the plants to grow well, you will need to remember they are living things, but to start with, you'll need to get the look right, and then concentrate on plant care.

When you are considering which plants to grow, write out or think in terms of a specification, rather than a plant name. For example, you may want a row of evergreen plants to grow to three metres high but no more than 60cm wide. Alternatively you may decide that your small garden needs a feature plant to give shade in summer and sun in winter, but that it must grow to no more than five metres tall and wide. Be as specific as you like: your local nursery will find a plant that fits the bill.

MULTI-TALENTED PLANTS

Another way of deciding which plants to grow in a small space is to demand that anything you grow is multi-talented. As well as asking if it suits your basic needs, also ask what else it can do. Consider its features, such as flowering time and impact, perfume, foliage colour, bark colour and fruit. A good plant choice >

small gardens: planning

SIDE PATHWAYS

Side passages have obvious physical limitations and many are neglected because of this. But they have their merits, too. They direct traffic, so should provide a stable walking surface and should feature plants that thrive in low light, such as clivias, begonias or hydrangeas. From within the house, a side passage should offer glimpses of green or interesting shapes. *Pavers frame a water feature and link the house with the garage (above). Pittosporum screens the boundary fence. A granite path runs along the length of this Japanese-inspired home (right). A planting of mature trees leads to a creek. An avenue of strategically lit and carefully underpruned tulip trees provides the structural form for this stylish passageway (opposite). Pavers set into a bed of river pebbles direct the eye to a massed planting of mondo grass. Terracotta limewashed walls contrast splendidly.*

< for a small garden would be one that is always offering something interesting, regardless of the season. Crab apple, for example, has spring flowers, colourful fruit and autumn leaves. Even when bare in winter, it will add a sculptural quality.

Thanks to the wonders of modern plant breeding and development, it is now possible to grow even productive plants like fruit trees in small spaces. Trees or shrubs that flower, fruit and have interesting leaves are going to be among the best multi-talented plants you can find for a small space.

Cumquats and 'Meyer' lemons, for example, readily lend themselves to being grown in containers. They bring year-round interest through their flowers, colourful and useful fruit, as well as their attractive and evergreen foliage. Also fitting the bill are 'Ballerina' apples and crab apples, a range of miniature fruit trees that grow wherever normal-sized apples and crab apples do – they just need less room. These plants are narrow, columnar fruit trees that can be enjoyed in a small garden as a living sculpture, a hedge or a feature plant. They also have >

VERTICAL PLANTS

Gardeners can sometimes get fixated at ground level – in the area of borders, ground covers, low shrubs and pot plants. Remember that there's another dimension to your garden – the vertical one. Climbing plants, tall hedges, hanging baskets and espalier are all elements to use when bringing life to this dimension. Screens or lattice are perfect for training twining plants towards the sky. Mandevilla is a good choice in many areas, particularly 'Alice du Pont' with its large, pink flowers. The misleadingly named Chilean jasmine (actually *Mandevilla laxa*) is a fast-growing, fragrant plant, which performs well in a pot if there isn't enough room in the ground. For jasmine fans, the summer-flowering *Jasminum officinale* will grow strong and tall. Wisteria provides a dense screen for privacy, or can be trained up and over a pergola or arbour for spectacular effect; being deciduous, it will let the sun through in winter. Rows of hanging baskets are perfect for a display above ground. Fill them with cascading plants, such as convolvulus, ivy geranium or Spanish shawl, for a screen. A fruit tree espaliered against a wall not only looks great, but makes the most of every centimetre for productivity.
A timber fence planted with redolent 'Golden Shower' roses (above) forms a backdrop to a water channel running through this NSW garden. The fragrance of star jasmine greets visitors by the gate (below left). Espaliered camellia and ficus create a striking pattern on a rendered wall (below right).

< interest throughout the year, with spring flowers and summer or autumn fruit and colour, before they shed leaves in winter.

The use of dwarfing rootstock and multigrafting has increased the range of citrus and other fruit trees that are small enough to grow in a small garden in the ground or in a large container.

TAKING CONTROL

The walls of a small space are such inviting areas for plants to grow that they often become overwhelmed with green stuff. Over-planted, they can bring all your planning undone. When it comes to plant choices, don't rush in with the fastest-growing climbing plant you can find. If you do, it won't be long before you're spending your entire spare time pruning. Rampant climbers, such as jasmine, on walls and other garden structures will also make the area seem smaller and more enclosed.

Consider a more refined scheme. Plants can be trained into wall decorations by the art of espalier. Espalier is fashionable, but it is also extremely practical and it sounds more complicated than it is. All the term means is growing a plant along one plane by training its branches along horizontal and vertical wires. Camellias, fruit trees, prostrate cotoneasters and even climbing plants such as star jasmine can be espaliered.

As the plants are literally trained into any shape or size that you want, espaliering a plant against a wall is a way of gaining control over a plant that would otherwise be too big or too boisterous for the space you have available. In its

simplest form, a suitable plant is placed in the middle of the area you want to cover and its branches or tendrils are trained by clipping and tying them onto a series of wires or a lattice screen fixed against the wall. You then retain and train vertical and horizontal growth and remove all outward-spreading growth.

TAMING PLANTS

As well as training plants to grow where and how you want them on a flat, vertical surface, you can also tame them with clipping and shaping them in the round. This is called topiary and can take the form of a simple 'lollipop' shape – round head on a stem – usually referred to as a standard, or more complex boxes, prisms or even animal shapes.

Simple or complex, standard plants and topiaries are the ideal plants for a small space. Not only are they clipped so they take up less room, standards are grown on a tall stem so that there's room beneath them to grow other plants. Almost any small-leafed plant can be trained as a standard or shaped by topiary. Good examples are lillypillies, camellias, azaleas, gardenias, oleanders, abutilon, daisies, roses and even lavender, but there are many more.

You can save yourself time by buying a topiarised plant from a nursery. Ask for tips on how to maintain it. All you need are sharp secateurs and a good eye. If you don't trust your eye, use a guide such as a string line for straight lines or a hoop to maintain a circular shape. Keep the plant tidy with light pruning, often referred to as a haircut, during the growing season.

Repetition looks good in this smaller garden (left) because it reinforces the structure of the space, avoiding the clutter of a lot of little pots. Low, bushy ornamental grasses, such as carex, are planted in plain terracotta pots with decorative rocks adding an earthy touch. You can have a garden at your doorstep when you plant in containers (opposite). These days people are more adventurous with their choice of pots and urns, but simple terracotta and stone containers are suitable for the French provincial look seen here. This miniature garden is clipped to keep it in bounds. Exuberant pots of bulbs and pansies add a seasonal highlight.

gardening in containers

When an outdoor space is small, there's always room for containers. As well as enabling gardening in small areas or on balconies high above ground level, containers have many benefits. They can be highly ornamental, provide custom-made growing conditions to suit the particular needs of whichever plants you want to grow, and they're mobile – a big plus if you're renting or on the move a lot.

BUYING THE BEST POT

When you head to the nursery or garden shop to buy a pot, you'll be overwhelmed at the huge variety on offer. Not only do pots come in every size, shape and colour

you can think of, they also come in a range of prices and materials. Containers in which to grow plants can be made of plastic, fibreglass, ceramic or terracotta (glazed or unglazed), stone, cement or even metal. They can be made of one material but styled to resemble another.

Indeed, they don't have to be purpose made – great containers can evolve from any recycled receptacle you come across, from an old boot to a worn-out wheelbarrow or even a hollow log.

So, what's your best choice? As a general rule, always go for the largest pot you can manage in your space. If you have room for more than one container, select >

Pinks and reds catch the eye in this cottagey display of pots, shrubs and ground covers (above). An old cut-down wine barrel makes a clever container for a fuchsia, which in turn is nestled into a bank of glorious hydrangeas. Stainless steel containers give a dramatic contemporary edge to a city apartment's balcony garden (opposite). Tall plaited trunks of Ficus longifolia, underplanted with impatiens and grouped in a single line, create a barrier to street noise, while offering privacy and protection from prevailing breezes.

< pots that match. Nothing looks more haphazard than a group of differently styled pots. A selection of the same style of pot in differing sizes, however, can be arranged together to form an attractive, multi-level garden.

When you've made your container selection, check for the following features before you hand over the money and take the pot to its new home.

Look at the shape and its potential stability: Pots that are tall and narrow or wider at the top than the base are more at risk of being blown or knocked over than a squat pot. The problem of instability only gets worse when a plant is added. If your garden is exposed to wind or the pots are likely to be knocked over, or you want to fill the pot with something that's tall or bushy, avoid unstable pots.

Consider the drainage: Unless you are selecting a pot for a water garden, all pots must have drainage holes in their bases. One small hole, or no hole, will mean poor drainage and, probably, dead plants. Check the base of the pot for drainage holes and if they're inadequate only buy the pot if you can drill extra holes. It is possible to drill a hole in most pots if you have the right drill and bit.   >

< What goes in must come out: If you are planning on changing the plant display without breaking the pot, select a pot that will allow for easy removal of its contents. It is very difficult to remove a plant with a large root ball from a pot with a narrow mouth or waist.

Glazed or unglazed: Unglazed pots, such as terracotta, lose water readily. This means the soil dries out quickly – which can be a big plus for succulents, but may spell certain death for less accommodating plants. Glazed pots usually retain moisture longer, are cooler and cause less stress to plants. To glaze an unglazed pot, you can seal it inside with a pot sealer.

Think about the weight: Remember pots have to be filled with potting mix and a plant. The larger the pot, the greater the amount of potting mix and the heavier the pot will be when it's planted up. If you want to keep things light and easy, go for plastic or fibreglass pots. If you live in a windy spot, the extra weight of a heavy, glazed ceramic pot may be a plus. Large or weighty pots should be put into position before you add potting mix to them, as they will be difficult to move later.

WHAT GROWS IN POTS?

Gardening books have a knack of making the task of putting a plant into a pot sound like hard work. It isn't. All you need is the pot, the plants to go into >

A captivating display of potted convolvulus, petunias and yellow dwarf marigolds adorn a painted wrought-iron love seat. These pot plants are set to catch the only patch of sun in the centre of a shaded garden.

ORIENTAL FEATURES

The trend for 'cocooning' in our homes that gathered pace in the late 1990s and continues today has seen complementary growing interest in the concept of 'Zen'. The philosophy of Zen Buddhism revolves around removing clutter, emphasising natural textures, and engaging restraint. These ideas of simple beauty are fulfilled to perfection in an Oriental garden, and it is for this reason that we have seen elements of such gardens creep into our own. Many people, in fact, have used these age-old principles to create brand-new Zen gardens – havens designed to help change their focus and concentrate peace within. There are several essential elements of design for such a garden.

Simple range of materials: Natural rock, sand or light-coloured pebbles, evergreen foliage for a sense of permanence, and perhaps one or two deciduous or flowering plants for contrast.

Enclosure: A simple backdrop against which to view the garden, closing it off from the complicated outside world.

Space: Vital on a philosophical level. An Oriental garden is never bursting with life, instead each element forms a space in which the visitor is encouraged to pause.

Asymmetrical balance: There is no one point in an Oriental garden that is dominant, instead many areas are designed to draw the eye. Japanese gardens, for example, use a triangle as the basis of design.

Harmony of nature and man: Neatly raked gravel, a beautifully carved water basin, neat walls and fence are all signs of man. They are juxtaposed with natural rocks, random tufts of grass, or a wandering stream, to show a harmonic relationship between nature and man.

Water: Whether running or still, water plays an important role.

Pathways: These are not designed to get from one place to another, but rather to wind through the garden, bringing attention to various features.

1 A classic Japanese wooden bridge built in red gum is reinforced with railway sleepers. 2 A Balinese-style lily pond. 3 Traditionally, a Japanese fish pond is shallow so that the fish are clearly visible. 4 A Balinese statue is an element of surprise in the lush greenery. 5 Bamboo spouts trickle water into a stone basin, giving equal emphasis to both sound and visual qualities.

LOOK TO THE TROPICS

Some regions of Australia are blessed (and cursed) with a hot, steamy climate. While European plants may suffer in the tropical and subtropical parts of our country, gardens designed for the environment thrive. The best tropical gardens combine striking colour, shade and, essentially, water. The idea is to surround yourself with as much refreshing greenery as possible and add the dramatic touches that only tropical plants such as strelitzia, orchids, bromeliads, frangipani and bougainvillea can give. The current fashion in tropical gardens is for a Balinese-style oasis, complete with outdoor pavilions/kitchens, seating areas, and a small pool. Decorative elements such as statuary, water bowls, umbrellas, sculpture and even coloured banners are extremely effective.

1 *Crotons.* 2 *Curculigo.*
3 *Cooktown orchid.* 4 *Cat's whiskers.* 5 Cordyline *'Apple Blossom'.* 6 Orchid. 7 *Lipstick palm.* 8 *Palm fronds.*
Not far from Byron Bay in NSW, this gorgeous tropical garden (above) is designed to cover up as much of the ground as possible to prevent invasion by the dreaded camphor laurel and lantana. Shasta daisies provide plenty of ground cover with the bonus of pretty white and gold flowers throughout summer.

< the pot, and some bags of potting mix. Select a potting mix that's tailor-made to suit your plant's growth or just a general purpose mix for containers.

If you are concerned that the 'dirt' may leak out through the drainage holes in the pot's base, simply cover the holes on the inside with a small piece of shade-cloth or mesh before you tip in the mix.

When you buy the pot, work out its volume in litres. To get the right amount of potting mix to fill that container,

divide the volume of the pot by 30, which is the volume in litres of an average bag of potting mix. A large trough may take five or six bags of potting mix to fill, whereas one bag of potting mix will fill eight small pots or hanging baskets.

While you're shopping for potting mix, it's also worth investing in slow-release fertiliser (select one for potted plants) and a bag of mulch for the surface of the pot. Choose either an organic mulch, such as pelletised lucerne hay, or >

SUCCULENT GARDEN

Low-maintenance, sculptural, no-fuss – succulents are popular contemporary plants for good reason. They thrive on neglect, so are perfect for the time-poor, and grow well in pots or in garden beds, making them a versatile option. Depending on the species, they can be used as a striking feature plant, or can be planted *en masse* to great effect. Most succulents come from hot, dry parts of the world, such as Mexico, Central America and Africa. They grow in well-drained sandy or gravel-based soils, enjoy a dry climate with low humidity, and tolerate hot summers and cold winters. In many parts of Australia, too much rain and long periods of humidity can lead to leaf rot, spots and fungal problems. They do enjoy some watering, particularly in spring, but should be kept fairly dry through winter.

Succulents look particularly good against weathered timber, tin or stainless steel, terracotta and pebbles. They range in shade from grey-green through to pink, yellow, orange, brown and even black, so are particularly useful for garden decoration. Some varieties, such as kalanchoes, are grown for flowers as well as foliage interest. If growing in pots, select a well-drained or specially designed cactus and succulent potting mix, and surround plants with gravel or pebbles. *This South Australian garden (opposite) features contrasting textures and plants adapted to a hot summer. The spiky leaves of a cabbage palm, Gymea lilies (Doryanthes excelsa) and agave contrast with other succulents, purple catmint and a potted yucca (Yucca constricta) to make a stunning display. Agave attenuata and Echeveria 'Black Prince' in a stone urn sit well in a formal courtyard (right).*

< an inorganic mulch such as small pebbles or gravel. The mulch protects the potting mix and makes it look more attractive.

Finally, elevate the pot slightly so it isn't sitting flat on the ground. Use pot feet, bricks or chocks to do this. This helps with drainage and prevents roots from growing into the ground.

GOOD WATERING

Correct watering is the most important part of caring for potted plants. On hot or windy days, pots may need daily watering, but a check below the surface of the potting mix will tell you if the plant is in need of a drink. If the container is standing in a saucer, empty the excess water from the saucer after watering.

If the water runs down the inside of the pot rather than soaking into the potting mix, the plant may be pot-bound – which means that the roots have filled up the space inside – or the potting mix may have dried so much it has become water-repellent. Pot-bound plants need to be repotted, but water-repellent potting mix can usually be made absorbent again with the help of a wetting agent.

POTS

Just about any plant can be grown in a pot given the right sized pot and the right blend of potting mix. Remember plants that grow in pots need more regular care and attention than the same plant in the ground, but most will keep looking good with regular water, liquid fertiliser and trimming or pruning to maintain their shape and size. Modern technology has made a huge difference to the ease of growing plants in pots. Free-draining potting mix means that crocks, or broken pieces of pots, are no longer required in the base of potted plants. In fact, adding crocks can impede drainage and adversely affect plant growth. Every two to three years, repot your plants into a slightly larger pot with fresh potting mix.

1. Petunias and marigolds turn a pot into a summer highlight. For winter and spring, change the planting to pansies or dwarf sweet peas. Other annuals that do well in pots include alyssum and lobelia.

2. Autumn crocuses (*Zephyranthes candida*), sometimes called storm lilies, grow well in pots and produce starry white flowers in late summer and autumn. They have tufty green leaves all year round. Start with a shallow pot and some small bulbs. Other bulbs that thrive in pots include hyacinths and tulips.

3. Lavenders, geraniums, herbs and vegetables can be moved around in their pots to find a sunny patch in a shaded garden. Pots can also be used where there is no room left to garden, or where the soil isn't suited to planting. Most herbs grow well in pots; you could try chives, basil or parsley.

4. Clipped lillypillies in a row of matching pots form a living screen next to an outdoor eating area. Pots of geraniums add a bold flash of red and accentuate the change in level. Potted plants, including citrus varieties such as cumquats and lemons, can be used as informal screens and to highlight entrances and paths.

5. Jelly bean sedum in a rustic pot sits nestled amid a ground cover of green foliage.

6. Aged pots in a shady spot may naturally develop a patina of green moss. To give new pots an aged look, paint them with yogurt and keep them moist – moss will soon follow.

7. House leeks and aeoniums form a cluster of succulents, making an effective, low-maintenance picture on this sunny table.

8. Pots have the real plus of being moveable. By putting a plant in a pot, you can grow anything just about anywhere. A potted plant is great to use as a highlight and to fill empty corners of your garden.

9. Clipped shrubs, such as this collection of topiarised box and lillypillies, are grown in pots for a stylish look in a small courtyard. Clipping and shaping plants helps to keep them in proportion to both their containers and the available space in a small area. These pots are kept well watered, as each has its own dripper attached to a watering system.

1

2

NATIVES

Native plants come in all shapes and sizes and bring colour, texture and scent to gardens. Many also attract birds and insects. If you grow native plants, you don't have to devote the entire garden to them. Many modern cultivars of Australian plants can be grown in gardens of all types and styles, from cluttered cottage gardens to stark, minimalist courtyards. If you want an all-native planting, consider growing plants that would occur naturally in your neighbourhood. These are called indigenous plants and have adapted to suit the needs of your particular soils and climate. Local councils and specialist plant societies will assist you in identifying the indigenous plants of your area.

1. The Sydney rock lily or rock orchid (*Dendrobium speciosum*) grows naturally on rock ledges along the east coast of Australia. It can be grown in gardens nestled under trees, positioned on a natural rock outcrop or attached to a backing board hung on a tree or a wall. But these plants do not grow buried in soil; they must be grown in a dendrobium mix, or a combination of bark and mulch. The glorious sprays of creamy yellow flowers appear in spring.

2. Lemon bottlebrush (*Callistemon pallidus*) is a white-flowered form of this common Australian native. Grow bottlebrush as specimen trees or screening plants. The flowers, which are seen mainly in spring, attract nectar-feeding birds and insects.

3. All banksias are evergreen. Their flowers are long lasting and many are followed by gnarled seed pods.

4. Wattles, for instance the silver wattle (*Acacia dealbata*) pictured, grow in all parts of Australia. Their golden fluffy blossoms are seen particularly in winter and spring.

5. *Eucalyptus caesia*, with its huge pinky red flowers, is among the most beautiful of all the flowering gum trees. It suits a mild climate with low summer humidity and is native to Western Australia. In the garden it forms a small, silver-leaved tree and will grow happily in a large pot.

6. Drumsticks (*Isopogon* spp) show the variety of shapes and forms of native flowers. These shrubs have ferny leaves, which disguise a prickly nature, and curious golden flowers that leave behind a seed head shaped like a drumstick.

7. Grevilleas come in two main varieties: spider-flower forms, as seen here, or those with toothbrush-shaped flowers. To encourage bushy growth, lightly prune grevilleas after a major flush of flowers.

8. Waratahs are not the easiest of natives to grow, but new varieties are making this spectacular plant more accessible to home gardeners. Cut flowers make long-lasting floral arrangements.

9. Kangaroo paw forms an impressive clump in a garden or a pot. The paw-shaped flowers attract nectar-feeding birds.

SMALL TREES

In a small space, choose trees with care. Be guided by their ultimate size, shape and what they have to offer your garden. The best choices are compact (under 10 metres tall), named varieties that won't overwhelm the available space. They should have flowers, a graceful shape and, where sunlight is at a premium, lose their leaves in autumn to allow the winter sun to stream through. Some may have attractive autumn foliage and develop decorative fruit or seed pods. Trees in small spaces act as living umbrellas. They provide a cool, shaded spot to sit and relax. If space permits, site a table and chairs in the leafy shade of a tree. Don't be afraid of pruning a tree to suit the space. Some trees can even be shaped like giant topiaries.

1. Dogwood is a classic small tree for a cool-climate garden. It has pink or white spring flowers, attractive autumn foliage and is bare in winter. Make the most of the woodland feel by underplanting with azaleas or spring-flowering bulbs such as bluebells.

2. Flowering crab apple (*Malus ioensis*) is an excellent choice for a cool to temperate climate garden. This small tree has exquisite spring flowers followed by small, ornamental fruits called crabs. Crab apples can be grown in a small courtyard or as a central feature of a spring garden.

3. Wattles are not always short-lived trees. In a cool, moist climate, the blackwood (*Acacia melanoxylon*) shown here grows as a tall, stately,

evergreen tree. In late winter to spring it has round puffballs of cream to light yellow flowers that hide among its long, deep-green leaves.

4. Frangipani needs a warm, frost-free climate. In warm climates it will be in flower for most of the year. In temperate climates it flowers from summer to autumn. The leaves are discarded in winter, leaving behind a bare sculpture of succulent grey branches. As well as the white-flowered form seen here, there are also pink, red, yellow and orange varieties. Plants grow readily from cuttings.

5. Magnolias in full flower are a spectacular feature of gardens from late winter to spring. They can be grown in cool microclimates in the subtropics

but are seen at their best in cool and temperate gardens. Here one is underplanted with a mass of Iceland poppies.

6. Citrus varieties are an excellent choice for a small, evergreen tree. As well as having handsome leaves and highly scented cream flowers, they also produce decorative and delicious fruit. Here a lemon tree is trained against a warm wall. Also suited to small areas are cumquats, limes, kaffir limes and mandarins.

7. *Grevillea* 'Moonlight' is one of many native trees that can be grown in a small garden.

8. Golden robinia (*Robinia pseudoacacia* 'Frisia') is a glorious small deciduous tree. Its golden leaves add a bright uplifting element among the darker green foliage.

Blue chalksticks (Senecio serpens), with their thick, succulent, blue-green leaves, thrive in this hot, sunny spot in Karkalla, a Victorian coastal garden (see also overleaf).

coast to country

visions

From the country to the coast, Australia is a land of contrasts and differing climates. Exotic hothouse blooms grow rampant in our sweltering north, while fragile natives endure the harshest Outback conditions. English-style cottage gardens transplant beautifully in our highland areas; autumn leaves fall in the cooler regions of our southern States. Our spectacular coastline gives rise to glorious cascading gardens, a testament to survival against sun and salt. The key to successful gardening in Australia is to understand your local conditions and to make the most of them. Each garden in this chapter is an outstanding example of this premise at work. While you immerse yourself in these vivid displays, consider the origins of our best-loved plant species.

COASTAL GARDEN

As you'd expect from a continent with a coastline stretching 36,735km and a relatively inhospitable interior, Australia features the full gamut of coastal gardens. In the far north, the climate is tropical, with distinct wet and dry seasons. Further down the coast, from north of Brisbane to NSW's Coffs Harbour, conditions are subtropical; south of there, and most of the way around the southern coastline of the country, the climate is temperate, with cooler, less humid conditions and more moderate rainfall. Gardeners on the far north-west coastline, however, experience very dry conditions, moving towards a tropical zone, but without the rainfall.

Fiona Brockhoff and David Swann's garden, Karkalla, in Sorrento, Victoria, is a fine example of how working with the climate produces an exceptional garden. On the blustery Mornington Peninsula, the garden is only six years old but looks more mature due to a 'take no prisoners' philosophy. Only the strong plants survive, such as the blue Echium candicans *and the bright green rosettes of aeoniums on these pages. To one side of the house (opposite below), a garden is landscaped with indigenous moonah (*Melaleuca lanceolata*), coastal she-oak (*Allocasuarina verticillata*) and cushion bush to merge with surrounding dunes. A display of glass bottles shows a touch of originality.*

new arrivals to an old land

THE FIRST FLEET

The First Fleet and the beginnings of white settlement in Australia not only brought a new and unfamiliar people to this land, but new plants and animals that would completely and utterly transform it. Europeans imported food plants; grains, fruit trees and seeds of plants that sustained them at home. The aim was survival and food plants were essential.

The extensive records of the First Fleet tell us what was carried and where it was loaded on the long, nine-month journey from England. The fleet traversed the globe from Tenerife in the Canary Islands, to Rio de Janeiro in Brazil, to the Cape of Good Hope on the southernmost tip of Africa and then on to Botany Bay, reflecting the origins of many of our garden plants over the next two centuries. The journey was hard on plants so seed alone was boarded in England. On board the *Sirius* were 274 bushels of vegetable seed. Among them were many that have only just been rediscovered by gourmets...

"Dwf [dwarf] marrow Peas; Field pease, fine Colwort [cabbage] Seed, Green Savoy, Long Orange carrot, fine early York Cabbage, Best Onion Seed, Spinage, Speckld Kidney Beans, Parsnip, Asparagus Seed, Red Beet, White Beet, Early cauliflower, Cellery, Celeriac, Prickly Cucumber, Cabbage Lettuce, Green Coss [cos], Selesia do [ditto] [Silesian lettuce], Curld Parsley, Nassturtion, Sorrell, Green Brocoli, White do [white broccoli], Mustard, Cress."

At Tenerife, the fleet took on fresh vegetables, including pumpkins and onions. Eight weeks later, they reached Rio de Janeiro, where they obtained various subtropical and tropical plants and seeds. The logs record the lists...

"Coffee, both seed and plant; Cocoa in the nut; Cotton seed; Banana – plant; Oranges, various sorts both seed and plant; Lemons, seed and plant; Guava, seed; Tamarind; Prickly pear, plant with cochineal on it; Eugenia, or pomme-rose (rose-apple), a plant bearing fruit in a shape like an apple, and having the flower and odour of a rose; Ipecacuanha – three sorts; Jalap."

The selection still seems exotic. Prickly pear was known as the cochineal fig. The red dye, cochineal, was obtained from a scale insect hosted by prickly pear and Governor Arthur Phillip's supply contained the valuable scale. Next to gold, it was one of the most valued exports from >

The kitchen/herb garden at Karkalla (above) is also a drying area. Limestone columns (opposite) by New Zealand sculptor Chris Booth seem like a natural occurrence amid the 'found treasures and recycling' philosophy espoused at Karkalla (see also previous pages). This creative, unintrusive space is often used to illustrate the ideal future direction for Australian gardens.

< Central America since no European dye came close to the quality of the colour produced. Spain maintained a monopoly on cochineal production for 250 years until 1777, when cactus pads containing scale were smuggled out of Mexico.

England had been excluded from direct trade in cochineal and its textile industry had suffered as a result. Obtaining supplies in 1787, so soon after, was akin to a mercantile coup in its time. Later, a different species of prickly pear (*Opuntia stricta*) would overrun vast kilometres of farming land until the introduction of the cactoblastis beetle.

There are some in the selection that are less familiar to us now. *Cephaelis ipecacuanha* was the source of ipecac, an emetic also used to treat amoebic dysentery, a common complaint in the insanitary conditions of the time. Jalap (*Ipomoea purga*) has a tuberous root with laxative qualities. It is a relative of the common morning glory (*I. indica*), now a serious weed on Australia's east coast. Rose apple is the name given to a member of the lillypilly family (*Syzygium jambos*) from South-East Asia and tropical Australia, of which magnificent mature specimens can still be seen in the Royal Botanic Gardens in Sydney. It may have travelled to South America via the East Indies, but the rose apple picked up in Rio was possibly the Brazil cherry (*Eugenia brasiliensis*) or a similar plant.

The fleet obtained pumpkins too, a vegetable of the Americas. The Brazilian ones grew prolifically when planted in the new colony. From them originated the particularly hard-shelled pumpkins, such as Ironbark or Queensland Blue, that have become popular in Australia. North American pumpkins and their hybrids generally have a softer skin.   >

SEASIDE GARDEN

One of the main benefits of coastal gardening is that such regions are frost-free. Problems, however, include salt spray, windy conditions and sandy soils. Preparation and forethought are key: soils must be constantly enriched with manure and compost, salt-tolerant plants are essential – consider creating living screens of such plants to protect less tolerant plants. *This colourful garden in the north-west of Tasmania incorporates lawn and richly hued flower borders that creep right to the edge of the sand (opposite). It was established 30 years ago, when piles of seaweed were used to add nutrients to the very sandy soil. Today, buffalo-grass lawns cut swathes through drifts of wallflowers, penstemons, poppies, nasturtiums and snapdragons. Drought-loving species in hot, primary colours are the backbone of this garden, although it does have a plentiful supply of fresh water piped from a dam a kilometre away. The owner's tip for seaside gardeners is to remember that plants grow fast but are short-lived, so their replacement must be planned. The garden is bold with spires of tiger lilies (top left), orange and yellow gaillardias (centre left), also known as blanket flowers, and the late-spring flowering red field poppies (bottom left), also known as Flanders poppy. Arctotis, also called aurora daisy, grows well by the sea (opposite).*

< THE LOVE APPLE

Surprisingly, tomatoes were not on the official First Fleet list, though they were soon present. As early as 1793, a visiting Spanish botanist, Don Luis Née, recorded seeing them growing in convict gardens west of Parramatta. It is likely that soldiers, on the First Fleet or later ships, privately procured seed while the vessels were restocking in Rio de Janeiro.

Along with other South American plants – corn, potato, sweet potato, capsicum, pumpkins, beans, tobacco and sunflowers – tomatoes were the real treasures of that continent. Then known as love apples, they arrived in Europe in the 16th century and herbalist John Gerard grew them in Britain as early as 1597. They failed to gain popularity, possibly due to the lack of summer heat. Sydney nurseryman Thomas Shepherd, in his 1835 lectures, suggested staking tomatoes as for peas and "they would produce excellent crops, much better than in England". Love apples only reached a level of popularity in England in the 1850s when a new name, 'tomato', gained currency.

The next stop for the First Fleet, the Cape of Good Hope, yielded fruiting plants and the first exotic ornamentals, myrtle and oak. Figs, sugar cane, vines including grapes, strawberries, apples, pears and quince were acquired. The Cape would continue to be a popular source of plant introductions in the centuries to follow, filling the gardens of Australia. Not only did southern Africa have a vast array of endemic flora, but it was also an established outpost of European settlement. As such, it served as a horticultural staging post.

Plants brought out with the pioneering First Fleet formed the origins of gardening and agriculture in Australia and the early results were pleasing. Governor Phillip recorded this in his journal...

"All the plants and fruit trees brought from Brazil and the Cape which were not damaged in the passage thrive exceedingly and vegetables have now become plentiful: both the European sorts and such as are peculiar to this country. In the Governor's garden are excellent cauliflowers and melons, very fine of their kinds. The orange trees flourish and the fig trees and vines still more rapidly. In a climate so favourable, the cultivation of the vine may be carried to any degree of perfection and… the wines of New South Wales may perhaps hereafter be sought with avidity and become an indispensable part of European tables." *

Governor Phillip's prophetic thought would not be realised for another two centuries. In the meantime, good yields in the gardens established on the notorious penal settlement on Norfolk Island supplemented the Farm Cove produce. Theft, drought and shipwrecks were to wreak havoc, though, in following years.

FRUIT TREES AND VINES

Apart from the plants arriving with the First Fleet, fruit and other edibles formed a major part of the plant imports well into the 19th century. Fruit trees and vines grew well in the young colony.

The quince that arrived with the First Fleet from the Cape of Good Hope eventually became a valued ornamental tree and fruit-bearer. Quinces were great survivors, often outlasting the early settlers, and they are still seen in old gardens, even today. Garden designer Edna Walling used quinces ornamentally as late as the 1930s in the Victorian garden, Boortkoi. Sir William Macarthur's Camden Park estate near Camden in New South Wales soon had one of the finest orchards in the colony. It still contains Australia's oldest-surviving apple tree, a Gravenstein, which was planted in 1837.   >

Kalanchoes and wallflowers thrive in the tough conditions of this Tasmanian seaside garden (see also previous pages). A layer of seaweed mulch added regularly is the secret ingredient in the success of this garden.

ROSE GARDEN

Beautiful rose gardens require certain conditions. A dry Mediterranean or cool climate is best, as humidity provides the perfect environment in which diseases thrive. The rose's key requirements are full sun, a well-drained soil, an open site in which air moves freely, and careful watering. Mulch is also important, and lucerne is an excellent choice, as research indicates that it helps combat the diseases to which roses are prone. Choosing wisely, by searching out the more resistant rose varieties, is another vital element for success.

A classic Edwardian garden is a combination of the formal and informal, and The Scented Rose, on the banks of the Huon River in Tasmania, certainly reflects that philosophy. A 30-metre-long border of David Austin roses (opposite) is interspersed with perennials such as clematis and foxgloves, while the rose walk (above) features standard David Austin roses, with climbing varieties rambling over the archways.

<   Nurseryman George Suttor, sent out to the colony in 1798 by Sir Joseph Banks, reported back in 1800...

"I do myself the honour of writing to you an account of what plants I have been able to take alive to New South Wales – 1 olive, 6 black mulberry, 6 white ditto, 4 willows, 18 chilly strawberries, 2 walnuts, 2 plantain, mint, and the following sort of vines – Tokery, White Muscadine, Constantia, and Muscat of Alexandria. It is with painful concern that I inform you, Sir, that I have not been able to bring the hops and many other valuable plants that I had on board."

In 1802, Suttor received a grant of land at Baulkham Hills, north-west of Sydney, in a region that would become the city's orchard district for more than two centuries, through until the present day, in fact. He was also presented with some rare orange trees, although his first crop of these would not be ready to go to market until 1807. In the meantime, he set up a nursery at Baulkham Hills and by 1804 was selling...

"A variety of young Fruit Trees, consisting of Apples, Pears, Early Peaches, Figs, Apricots, a few Almonds, of a particularly fine sort from the Cape, Pomegranates, Lemons, Locusts, Raspberry, large Chilly Strawberries, Quinces, Willows, Etc."   >

COUNTRY GARDEN

Country gardens need to be attuned to climatic conditions more than most. Drought strikes harder in Australia's rural areas, so plants are best chosen for their water-wise qualities. Most inland inhabitants face hot, dry conditions, akin to a Mediterranean climate, in summer. Box and similar hedging plants (such as escallonia or *Viburnum tinus*) add structure and soothing verdancy in drier gardens during these days. English-style country gardens rely heavily on roses and borders of hardy perennials, such as the many forms of salvia, penstemon, yarrow, coneflower and marmalade daisy, for interest from late spring to autumn. *Clipped box hedges (left) provide the framework for this country garden in a pastoral district of the NSW South Coast. Created over a 30-year period, the garden at Glencoe covers around two hectares of this 10-hectare property. The owners' passion for Italy has led to a Tuscan influence in areas of the garden. Crushed stone, urns and topiary (opposite above) are offset by borders of red-hot pokers, Gymea lilies, dietes and other plants above the lake. Cottage-style plants, such as salvia with its blue spires (opposite, below left) and the tall heads of the shade-loving Acanthus mollis (opposite, below right), bring long-lasting flowers to the borders.*

< THE FIRST ORNAMENTALS

Flower gardens in these early colonial days were a luxury. Even so, a few easy-to-grow perennials arrived, probably picked up by free settlers or soldiers as they sojourned at southern Africa's Cape of Good Hope. Among these first ornamentals were geraniums, more properly known as pelargoniums, that were drought hardy, salt tolerant and partially succulent, and so were well able to survive a long sea journey in poor conditions. Arthur Bowes-Smyth, ship's surgeon of the convict ship, *Lady Penryhn*, wrote this in his journal...

"Jany 1788. 5th. A very fine breeze. This night was so very hot that I was oblig'd to throw off the bedcloathes – There are now in the cabin Geraniums in full blossum and some grapevines which flourish very much, there are also Myrtles, Bananas and other sort of plant brot from Rio de Janeiro."

The first geranium to be brought to Australia was probably the rose-scented geranium (*Pelargonium capitatum*), which even today is naturalised around Captain James Cook's first landing spot of Botany Bay. Later, Captain William Kent would write this in the early 1800s... >

Box hedging, manicured lawns and lavender-lined paths, such as those extending from the guest quarters (opposite, above left), supply a cohesive structure to the garden at Glencoe (see also previous pages). Made up of many different 'rooms', including a formal front garden, potager, orchard, cottage garden and a trout-filled lake surrounded by red-hot pokers (opposite below) and dietes (opposite, above right), the garden has been successfully established despite harsh conditions such as strong westerly winds, high temperatures and a lack of mains water. Today, the sandstone-edged lake has been re-lined and is fed by catchment rain water, which is used to irrigate the property. Small touches, such as the chicken sculpture by Folko Kooper (right), are not overlooked in the grand scale of the garden.

< "Geraniums flourish in such abundance, that in various parts of the settlement, they are made into hedges, and are so thick as to be impenetrable; they are always in leaf and flower and emit an odour of the most fragrant nature, perfuming the surrounding atmosphere."

These hedges may have been a combination of the rose-scented geranium and the purple-flowered parent of the regal pelargonium, *P. cucullatum.*

A lady by the name of Mrs Charles Meredith, who resided in the colony in the 1840s, was, however, less than kind to the blossoming geranium stock...

"Geraniums thrive and grow rapidly but I did not seen any good ones; none that I would have thought worth cultivating in England. A Horticultural Society has been established some years now and doubtless they will be the means of much improvement."

By 1850, the Royal Horticultural Society of Victoria had awarded a prize to a display of 50 varieties of 'geraniums'. By the 1860s, Michael Guilfoyle's nursery in Sydney was listing 35 cultivars.

Their ability to survive with little water and their ease of propagation made geraniums popular in the colony. Henry

Lawson's touching story of hardship and loneliness among settler women, *Water Them Geraniums,* portrayed the stoic, hardy geranium as a symbol of strength and survival...

"Geraniums were the only flowers I saw grow in the drought out there. I remembered this woman had a few dirty grey-green leaves behind some sticks... and in spite of the sticks the fowls used to get in and scratch beds under the geraniums and scratch dust over them, and ashes were thrown there – with an idea of helping the flowers, I suppose."

Pelargoniums are popular to this day. >

< CENTURIES OF DISCOVERY

Sir Joseph Banks, whose role in the settlement in New South Wales was pivotal, exercised enormous influence and proposed a two-way trade in plants. England was the centre of the burgeoning trade in and exploration for new species by the hardy individuals who came to be known as 'plant hunters'.

The Romans had introduced many plants to Britain, but from about 1560 until 1620 plant arrivals came from Turkey, Asia Minor and southern Europe. Prior to 1687, plants began arriving from the Americas. Over a broad span of years, the North American colonies sent back plants such as the calico bush (*Kalmia latifolia*), *Rhododendron* species, perennial phlox and bergamot as well as Michaelmas and marmalade daisies to England. Other imperial powers received plants from their respective colonies. Spain imported the tomato, potato, beans and sweet potato for the table and sunflower, zinnia, dahlia, fuchsia, nasturtium, salvia, canna and other exotic beauties for the flower garden.

Between 1687 and 1771, the Dutch in South Africa sent to Europe daisies such as gerbera and dimorphotheca, >

TROPICAL GARDEN

Big leaves, big rainfall, steamy heat and bold flowers are the signatures of the tropical garden. In the tropics, summer is the wet season and winter the dry period. Many tropical plants have adapted to long periods without rain, flowering early in the winter period and using summer as a time for growth. In inland monsoonal areas, some gardens can be dry for six months of the year. These areas may even have frost on winter nights.

Cool greens and splashes of colour typify the essence of the tropical garden in this small suburban space in Deception Bay, Queensland. Abundant foliage is provided by plants such as cordylines, fan-leaf palms, bamboo, cycads and vireya rhododendrons, with extra colour added through painted feature walls. Changes of texture underfoot – from timber to gravel, for example – increase the feeling of space. Plantings alongside the walkway include cordyline, dracaena, croton, anthurium, assorted palms and many Duranta 'Sheena's Gold'.

In another area of the Deception Bay garden (see also previous pages), painted columns viewed down a weathered path are designed to add a feeling of age – think jungle ruins! Crotons and vireya rhododendrons add vibrant colour (above right).

< numerous bulbs including gladiolus, pelargoniums, red-hot pokers (*Kniphofia* species), impatiens, calla lilies and bird of paradise plants (*Strelitzia reginae*). This was Australia's horticultural legacy.

When Captain Cook returned to England with the first plant specimens from the east coast of Australia in 1772, a rage developed for these exotic natives that lasted until 1820. The Royal Botanic Gardens at Kew in south-west London were awash with plants from Australasia, and many flourished and flowered even when little was known of the natural habitat of the plants themselves, a testament to the skill of their gardeners. Most had to be grown under glass as they were not frost hardy, a factor which ultimately prevented many Australian plants from becoming internationally popular.

From 1820 until the turn of the century, wealthy aristocrats and merchants developed stove houses or heated greenhouses. These structures fanned the popularity of plant species discovered in tropical America, Africa and South-East Asia. Around this time, too, Japan and China were opened to the West and myriad hardy plants from these regions – camellias, rhododendrons, wisteria, lilies, peonies and chrysanthemums – flooded into Europe.

STOCKING THE COLONY

At the same time as the new antipodean colony was being established, plants were arriving in England from all over the world, first to stock the Gardens at Kew, then on to nurserymen who propagated and popularised these latest gems of the garden. Soon they would find their way to Sydney and the new colony.   >

AUTUMN FOLIAGE

Beautiful autumn foliage gardens are restricted to the cooler southern and mountain areas of Australia. Only there do we find the ideal conditions of cool nights and sunny days in autumn for the gradual retreat of chlorophyll (which keeps leaves green) and the isolation of other pigments, like carotin and anthocyanin, to produce the brilliant yellow, orange or red tones. It is worth making the most of deciduous colour if you have the right conditions. *Glen Rannoch, in Victoria's Mount Macedon, is a classic hill-station garden, designed in the late 19th century as a shady sanctuary for colonial gentry from Melbourne's summer heat. Trees feature here, particularly deciduous species such as ash, birch, beech and tupelo, while enormous conifers, including spruce, hemlock, a Ponderosa pine and monkey puzzle (Araucaria araucana), have grown to maturity among the eucalypts. A radiant maple and hoheria shield the cottage (left); the garden includes both Japanese maple (Acer palmatum) and red maple (Acer rubrum).*

< In 1789, the *Guardian*, the supply ship of the Second Fleet, set sail with two years' supplies for the colony, but with a brief to collect 150 of the finest fruit trees at the Cape of Good Hope. The ship struck an iceberg after leaving the Cape and was lost with all its provisions. Fortunately, another ship, the *Gorgon*, arrived in 1791 with supplies, 200 fruit trees and a quantity of garden seed.

THE BOTANIC GARDENS

Governor Lachlan Macquarie founded the botanic gardens of Sydney in 1816 as part of the Governor's Domain. At first, the land at Farm Cove was a means of feeding the colony, with areas devoted to cereals and vegetables. From their inception, the Sydney botanic gardens were used to acclimatise and assess new plants. (The acclimatisation beds can still be found today behind the Macquarie Wall, built to deflect salt-laden winds from the harbour and to separate the convict domain from the respectable citizens of Sydney.) Later, 'societies' devoted solely to introducing commercially valuable plants (and animals) sprang up in every colony and played a major, if not always beneficial, role. To them we owe the introduction of many useful crops, as well as noxious weeds that have wreaked havoc in the bush and notorious pests, such as rabbits, starlings, Indian mynahs, blackbirds and foxes, that have decimated native animal populations.

Macquarie had in mind the building of a major scientific establishment. Our long history of collection and study of plants began with the appointment of the first Colonial Botanist, Charles Fraser, in 1817. Fraser established valuable contacts with fellow Scots, particularly the director of the Edinburgh botanic garden, and also with the Danish-born director of the Calcutta botanic gardens, Dr Nathaniel

Wallich. Both gardens were centres of excellence in botany and horticulture and these connections made a great contribution to the development of Sydney's botanic gardens. By 1825, Fraser had introduced 3000 new food plants and fruit trees to the colony of New South Wales. In time, as other colonies around Australia grew, each capital city established its own botanic gardens: Hobart in 1818, Brisbane in 1828, Melbourne in 1846 and Adelaide in 1855.

THE FLOWER GARDEN

Sir Joseph Banks was not only instrumental in importing our food plants; he also fostered ornamental horticulture. In 1798, Banks purchased seeds for despatch to the colony. The collection listed below was indicative of the first ornamental flowers grown in the colony.

"34 annuals at 6d." These included what we would call common cottage flowers – cockscomb, convolvulus, larkspur, stock, chrysanthemum and aster.

"54 annuals at 3d." The cheaper price reflected the ease of growing these – calendula, candytuft, heart's ease, nasturtium, sunflower and antirrhinum.

"35 sorts of biennials and perennials." Among these were Canterbury bell, hollyhock, polyanthus, primrose, sweet scabious and sweet William.

Governor Philip Gidley King compiled a 'List of Plants in the Colony of New South Wales that are not indigenous, March 20th, 1803.' Many of those listed above are there but so too are wallflower, columbine, rose campion, goat's rue, lupin, *Canna indica*, mignonette, love lies bleeding (*Dicentra spectabilis*), Indian pink, balsam, larkspur and tobacco plants. The list did not include lavender or rosemary, although Banks' papers record that he recommended lavender, laurel and sweetbay "for garden plants" >

Beech leaves cover a mossy bank outside the stable at Glen Rannoch (see also previous pages). Planted in the 19th century, this tree is one of the garden's original specimens. Much of the garden was damaged in the 1983 Ash Wednesday bushfires and a policy of careful revitalisation is still underway. Cool, dark, mysterious walks are a feature of this style of garden, and the three-hectare property is linked by these and the 568 steps that allow access to all levels.

WOODLAND GARDEN

Cool and misty mountain ranges are the ideal place for a woodland garden. Tall trees shade the ground, keeping soil cool, while falling leaves and constant moisture ensure a rich dressing of natural humus to nourish smaller plants.

Cold, frosty winters with the occasional snowfall invigorate cool-climate plants, so select frost- and cold-hardy ones. Spring is the main flowering season in the cool mountain garden, when plants jump from dormancy to a blaze of new foliage and brilliant flowering. Summer, in contrast, is a period of relative calm on the flower front while autumn provides a second season of spectacle as foliage turns to rich tones of yellow, orange and red.

Wanawong, a one-hectare garden in Victoria's Otway Ranges, is a cool-climate spectacular. In spring, the garden is in full bloom, with vireya rhododendrons, bulbs, azaleas and rare alpine plants providing an effusive display. Deciduous trees provide shade in summer and a russet canopy for cyclamen, lapageria and roses in autumn.

BUSH GARDEN

A bush garden is generally found in temperate parts of the country with reasonably good annual rainfall. Many native plants are adapted to the climate and soil of a particular region. For example, plants native to colder mountain areas, or to the well-drained sands of south-west Western Australia, seldom thrive on the hot and humid east coast. Once plants are established, a bush garden can survive on the natural rainfall, making it the most environmentally acceptable of all garden types. All that is needed is general maintenance, such as pruning, weeding and mulching. Structure comes from blending trees and shrubs for foliage, pattern and texture contrasts. With only a few flowering perennials in the Australian palette, the colour comes mostly from flowering shrubs and ground covers. Late winter is the main flowering season for many natives but, with care and planning, there can be colour, as well as nectar for native animals and birds, all year. Bottlebrushes flower in spring and autumn, while many grevilleas are never without blooms. Use kangaroo paw and brachyscome daisies for long-term colour patches. *Stands of gums and native shrubs are interspersed with meandering paths in this native bush garden, Montrose, near Melbourne. Part of a 2.5-hectare property, the garden blends naturally into the surrounding vegetation. The owners have grouped plants that would grow together naturally; there are almost 1000 native species, including 60 eucalpyts, 50 grevilleas and 20 hakeas. On the front path (opposite),* Eucalyptus leucoxylon *(dark trunk) and* Eucalyptus ovata *stand guard.*

< as early as 1798 and they would have arrived some time shortly afterwards.

Equally popular were roses. The Cape of Good Hope is the likely source for the first colonial roses. The Dutch colonists who were living there gleefully recorded the first bloom of the Provence rose, *Rosa x centifolia*, in 1659 and it was Dutch rose growers who, 300 years ago, first developed this complex hybrid. It is unlikely roses arrived with the First Fleet, but they were already popular in the colony around 1800. After the first decade of settlement, plants, and presumably roses, were arriving with each new ship in such quantities that Governor King in 1803 listed in his despatches to London three exotic plants plentiful in the new colony – the geranium, the sweet briar and the Provence rose.

The briar or dog rose (*Rosa canina*), a wild rose sometimes used as rootstock, rapidly took off and is now weedy in cold winter regions. In Europe at this time, roses were experiencing a surge in popularity following the introduction of *Rosa chinensis* which brought repeat flowering to European hybrids. Among the early popular China roses were 'Lady Brisbane' and 'Old Blush'. By 1850, however, Sir William Macarthur had listed more than 70 varieties at Camden Park.

THE COLLECTORS

Sir William Macarthur published extensive catalogues from 1843 onwards and from them it is possible to glean how incestuous botanical collecting had become. For instance, he obtained plants from Dr Wallich in India, who supplied >

The natural-looking pond (left and opposite) was developed by the owners soon after they purchased this bush property (see also previous pages). It is edged with tussocks of creeping rush (Restio tetraphyllus), while everlasting daisies (Chrysocephalum baxteri) line the path. The stand of Eucalyptus leucoxylon (opposite), is underplanted with Grevillea montis-cole (a variety from Mount Cole, Victoria). Native plants, such as Epacris longiflora (opposite below left) and Anigozanthos 'Bush Ranger' (opposite below right) require little fertilisation and should never be mulched with still-green grass or fresh manure, which will generate too much heat and damage delicate roots.

< British gardens and large London nurseries. The nursery of Conrad Loddiges occupied six hectares in Hackney and was a principal source for Macarthur gardens. They too sent collectors into the field around the world and thus 19th-century Australian gardeners were hooked into the collecting merry-go-round.

Already a noted amateur naturalist, Alexander Macleay arrived in Australia as Colonial Secretary under Governor Sir Ralph Darling in 1825. Macleay developed a private botanical garden at his home, Elizabeth Bay House, importing many now-common species. His notes often include the annotation "dead" beside entries of plants from South Africa. Importation was a hazardous business, dependent on the interest of the captain, the horticultural expertise of the crew, and the weather conditions.

The invention of an enclosed glass case by Nathaniel Ward in 1829 changed all this. Known as the Wardian case, this portable greenhouse made plant movement easier. The first test of the new system came with plant transports to New South Wales in the early 1830s. It passed with flying colours. Wardian cases soon became a fashion statement in well-to-do Sydney homes.

FAMILIAR FAVOURITES

Plants continued to be introduced for many reasons, not the least of which was some degree of nostalgia. A famous lithograph entitled 'A primrose from England' showed English primroses arriving at the docks with supposedly homesick colonials swooning over them. In truth, it depicted the blaze of publicity shown at the excellent condition of plants transported in Wardian cases. Familiar English plants were arriving and were being grown, but when the climate eventually overtook the cold-loving plants of Europe, hotter climate varieties, such as Spanish bluebells, were substituted for the English form.

After the 1830s, plant introductions were orderly and consistent. Sir William Macarthur's plant catalogues of 1843 indicate that most of the major plant groups were already well established in the new colony, at least in selected private gardens. By the 1850s, nursery catalogues of the times show most plants now commonly grown were already available to the public. Researchers, including Victor Crittenden and Dr Richard Clough, have detailed the lists of nurseries in the 19th century, and the period's interest in fuchsias, camellias, early rose varieties and flowers like gladiolus and pelargonium can be readily seen.

The late 19th century was an exciting and tumultuous time for plant collectors, with new species being discovered yearly. Organised expeditions funded by European nurseries and botanic gardens regularly set off to South America, Asia and Africa. Their bounty, of course, first found its way to England, America, France or Germany, depending on the sponsorship, but soon these discoveries were en route for Australian shores to provide us with the rich horticultural heritage that we all enjoy today.

acknowledgments

CODE
A=Architect; **BO**=Bottom; **GD**=Garden Designer; **L**=Left; **LD**=Landscape Designer; **P**=Photography by; **PD**=Pool Designer; **R**=Right; **T**=Top; **TL**=Top Left; **TR**=Top Right.

FRONT COVER P: Ray Joyce.
GD: Elaine Rushbrooke, The Scented Rose, Glaziers Bay, Tasmania.
Pg 2 P: Leigh Clapp.
Pg 5 P: Leigh Clapp.
Pg 6 P: Leigh Clapp.

TODAY'S GARDENS
Pg 8 P: Leigh Clapp. **GD:** Darryl Mappin Garden Design, Brisbane, Qld.
Pg 10 1. P: Bill Anagrius. **A:** Kerry Fyfe, Monckton Fyfe, Sydney, NSW.
Pg 11 2. P: Trevor Fox. **A:** Nic Bochsler, Bochsler & Partners, Melbourne.
3. P: Dan Magree. Painting 'Barcelona' by Robert Jacks.
Pg 12 4. P: Trevor Mein. **LD:** Justin Hutchison Design, Melbourne, Vic.
Pg 13 5. P: Dan Magree. **6. P:** Lorna Rose.
Pg 14 7. P: Dan Magree. **8. P:** Simon Griffiths.
Pg 15 9. P: Dan Magree. **LD:** Jeanette Strachan, Balwyn North, Vic.
Pg 16 10. P: Leigh Clapp. **GD:** Darryl Mappin Garden Design, Brisbane, Qld.
11. P: Leigh Clapp.
Pg 17 12. P: Dan Magree.

FRONT GARDENS
Pg 18 P: Leigh Clapp. **GD:** Lambley Nursery, Ascot, Vic.
Pg 20 P: Leigh Clapp. **GD:** Peter Fudge Garden Design, Sydney, NSW.
Pg 21 P: Dan Magree.
Pg 22 P: Wayne Miles. **A:** Architects Studio, Darwin, NT.
Pg 23 P: Leigh Clapp. **GD:** Peter Fudge Garden Design, Sydney, NSW.
Pg 24 P: Dan Magree.
Pg 25 T. P: Leigh Clapp. **GD:** Ann Marie Barkai, Rock 'n' Root Art Landscape and Design, Sunshine Coast, Qld.
BO. P: Nigel Noyes.
Pg 26 P: Dan Magree.
Pg 27 P: Andrew Elton.
Pg 29 P: Eric Victor-Perdraut. **GD:** Dig-it Landscapes, Brisbane, Qld.
WHICH STYLE? Pg 30 P: Dan Magree.
ENTRANCES & FENCES Pg 31
1. P: Simon Kenny. **2. P:** Dan Magree.
3. P: David Young. **4. P:** Dan Magree.
5. P: Dan Magree.
COLOUR Pg 32 L. P: Wayne Miles.
R. P: Joe Filshie.
PATHWAYS Pg 33 1. P: Leigh Clapp.
2. P: Leigh Clapp. **3. P:** Leigh Clapp.
4. P: Leigh Clapp.

FRONT GARDENS PLANT GUIDE
COTTAGE GARDENS Pg 34
1. P: Leigh Clapp. **2. P:** Leigh Clapp.
3. P: Leigh Clapp. **4. P:** Dan Magree.
5. P: Leigh Clapp.
ANNUALS Pg 35 6. P: Leigh Clapp.
7. P: Leigh Clapp. **8. P:** Leigh Clapp.
9. P: Leigh Clapp. **10. P:** Leigh Clapp.
SCULPTURAL Pg 36 1. P: Leigh Clapp.
2. P: Leigh Clapp. **3. P:** Leigh Clapp.
4. P: Leigh Clapp.
Pg 37 5. P: Leigh Clapp. **6. P:** Leigh Clapp. **7. P:** Ivy Hansen. **8. P:** Ivy Hansen. **9. P:** Dan Magree.

BACK GARDENS
Pg 40 P: Dan Magree. **GD:** Evan Gaulke, Ochre Landscape, Melbourne, Vic.
Pg 41 P: Dan Magree.
Pg 42 P: Lisa Cohen.
Pg 43 P: Simon Griffiths.
Pg 45 P: Robert Frith.
Pg 46 P: Trevor Fox.
Pg 47 P: Jennifer Soo.
Pg 48 PD: Coolibah Landscape Planners, Kangaroo Point, Qld.
Pg 49 P: Dan Magree.
Pg 50 P: Simon Kenny. **D:** Thomas Hamel, Woollahra, NSW.
Pg 51 P: Leigh Clapp.
Pg 53, 54, 55 P: Jeff Kilpatrick.
GD: Rick Eckersley, Eckersley Stafford Design, Richmond, Vic.
Pg 56 P: Valerie Martin.
Pg 57 P: Dan Magree.
Pg 58 P: Trevor Fox.
THE FAMILY GARDEN Pg 59
1. P: Leigh Clapp. **2. P:** Leigh Clapp.
3. P: Leigh Clapp. **4. P:** Leigh Clapp.
EXTENDING DAY INTO NIGHT Pg 60
1. P: Eric Victor-Perdraut. **2. P:** Eric Victor-Perdraut.
Pg 61 3. P: Eric Victor-Perdraut.
4. P: Eric Victor-Perdraut. **5. P:** Eric Victor-Perdraut. **6. P:** Eric Victor-Perdraut.
7. P: Andrew Elton. **8. P:** Andrew Elton.
Pg 62 P: Amanda McLauchlan. **GD:** Good Manors Landscaping, Sydney, NSW.
Pg 63 1. P: Simon Kenny. **2. P:** Simon Kenny. **3. P:** Dan Magree.

BACK GARDENS PLANT GUIDE
POOLSIDE Pg 64 1. P: Dan Magree.
2. P: Leigh Clapp. **3. P:** Eric Victor-Perdraut. **4. P:** Leigh Clapp. **5. P:** Leigh Clapp. **6. P:** Leigh Clapp.
Pg 65 7. P: Eric Victor-Perdraut.
8. P: Leigh Clapp. **9. P:** Leigh Clapp.
10. P: Leigh Clapp. **11. P:** Leigh Clapp.
SUCCULENTS Pg 66 1. P: Lorna Rose.
2. P: Leigh Clapp. **3. P:** Leigh Clapp.
Pg 67 4. P: Lorna Rose. **5. P:** Leigh Clapp. **6. P:** Dan Magree. **7. P:** Lorna Rose. **8. P:** Lorna Rose.
KIDS' BACK GARDEN Pg 68 1. P: Leigh Clapp. **2. P:** Rodney Weidland. **3. P:** Leigh Clapp. **4. P:** Leigh Clapp. **5. P:** Trisha Dixon.
Pg 69 6. P: Trisha Dixon. **7. P:** Leigh Clapp. **8. P:** Trisha Dixon.

INFLUENCES
Pg 70 P: Ivy Hansen. **GD:** Annette Irish, Whiteside, Qld.
Pg 72, 73 P: Ivy Hansen.
Pg 74, 75 P: Leigh Clapp.
Pg 76, 77 P: Richard Powers.
Pg 78, 79 P: Nigel Noyes.
Pg 80, 81 P: Eric Victor-Perdraut.
GD: Phillip O'Malley Garden Design, Pomana, Qld.
Pg 82, 83 P: Nigel Noyes.
Pg 84, 85 P: Chris Bennett.
Pg 87 P: Leigh Clapp. **GD:** Christine Elsbury, Sydney, NSW.
Pg 88 P: Nigel Noyes.
Pg 89 P: Leigh Clapp.
Pg 90 P: John Best. **GD:** Justin Hutchison, Melbourne, Vic.

CONSERVATORIES Pg 91 P: Andre Martin.
Pg 92 P: Trevor Fox.
Pg 93, 94 P: Nigel Noyes.
LAWN ALTERNATIVES Pg 95
1. P: Leigh Clapp. **2. P:** Trisha Dixon.
3. P: Joe Filshie. **4. P:** Lorna Rose.
5. P: Trisha Dixon. **6. P:** Leigh Clapp.
7. P: Leigh Clapp. **8. P:** Lorna Rose.
ORNAMENTAL GRASSES Pg 96, 97
P: Leigh Clapp. **GD:** Michael Cooke, Avant Garden, Gosford, NSW.

INFLUENCES PLANT GUIDE
CLIMBERS Pg 98 1. P: Leigh Clapp.
2. P: Dan Magree. **3. P:** Leigh Clapp.
4. P: Leigh Clapp. **5. P:** Trevor Fox.
WATER PLANTS Pg 99 6. P: Trisha Dixon. **7. P:** Leigh Clapp. **8. P:** Leigh Clapp. **9. P:** Leigh Clapp. **10. P:** Leigh Clapp. **11. P:** Leigh Clapp.
SCREENING Pg 100 1. P: Ivy Hansen.
2. P: Leigh Clapp. **3. P:** Leigh Clapp.
4. P: Leigh Clapp. **5. P:** Leigh Clapp.
6. P: Leigh Clapp. **7. P:** Leigh Clapp.
LAWNS Pg 101 8. P: Ivy Hansen.
9. P: Phil Aynsley. **10. P:** Nigel Noyes.
11. P: Ivy Hansen. **12. P:** Ivy Hansen.
13. P: Ivy Hansen. **14. P:** Ivy Hansen.
15. P: Ivy Hansen.

PERSONAL GARDENS
Pg 102 P: Nigel Noyes.
Pg 104, 105, 106 P: Nigel Noyes.
Pg 108, 109 P: Leigh Clapp. Sculptures by Folko Kooper and Maureen Craig, Rural Design, Oatlands, Tasmania.
Pg 110, 111 P: Nigel Noyes.
LOOKING AFTER YOURSELF IN THE GARDEN Pg 112 P: Nigel Noyes.
Pg 113 P: Eric Victor-Perdraut.
Pg 114, 115 P: Andrew Payne.
Pg 116, 117 P: Nigel Noyes.
Pg 118, 119 P: Nigel Noyes.
Pg 120, 121 P: Robyn Powell. **GD:** Peter Nixon, Paradisus, Sydney, NSW. Sculpture by Chris Bennetts, Ishi Buki, Sydney, NSW.

PERSONAL GARDENS PLANT GUIDE
VEGETABLES Pg 122 1. P: Leigh Clapp.
2. P: Nigel Noyes. **3. P:** Leigh Clapp.
4. P: Leigh Clapp. **5. P:** Leigh Clapp.
Pg 123 6. P: Leigh Clapp. **7. P:** Jeff Kilpatrick. **8. P:** Leigh Clapp.
9. P: Leigh Clapp.
HERBS Pg 124 1. P: Leigh Clapp.
2. P: Leigh Clapp. **3. P:** Leigh Clapp.
4. P: Leigh Clapp.
Pg 125 5. P: Leigh Clapp. **6. P:** Trisha Dixon. **7. P:** Leigh Clapp. **8. P:** Leigh Clapp. **9. P:** Trisha Dixon. **10. P:** Leigh Clapp.
FRAGRANT PLANTS Pg 126
1. P: Leigh Clapp. **2. P:** Leigh Clapp.
3. P: Trisha Dixon. **4. P:** Lorna Rose.
5. P: Leigh Clapp. **6. P:** Leigh Clapp.
7. P: Leigh Clapp.
Pg 127 8. P: Trevor Fox. **9. P:** Leigh Clapp.

SMALL GARDENS
Pg 128, 130 P: Trevor Fox. **LD:** Geoff Heppner, Accent Landscapes, Adelaide, SA.

Pg 131 P: Dan Magree.
Pg 132 P: Jeff Kilpatrick.
Pg 133 P: Trevor Fox. **A:** Christine Teichert, Archicentre, Adelaide, SA.
Pg 134 P: Lorna Rose.
Pg 135 P: Simon Griffiths. **GD:** Paul Bangay Garden Design, Melbourne, Vic.
Pg 136 P: Dan Magree.
Pg 137 P: Nigel Noyes.
SIDE ALLEYS Pg 138 L. P: Andre Martin. Pot by Robbie Harmsworth.
R. P: Leigh Clapp.
Pg 139 P: Simon Kenny. **GD:** Peter Fudge Garden Design, Sydney, NSW.
VERTICAL PLANTS Pg 140 T. P: Lorna Rose. **BO. L. P:** Leigh Clapp.
BO. R. P: Leigh Clapp.
Pg 142 P: Leigh Clapp.
Pg 143 P: Dan Magree.
Pg 144 P: Leigh Clapp. **GD:** Inside Out Urban Gardens, Sydney, NSW.
Pg 145 P: Leigh Clapp.
Pg 146 P: Nigel Noyes.
ORIENTAL FEATURES Pg 147
1. P: Trevor Fox. **2. P:** Leigh Clapp.
3. P: Leigh Clapp. **4. P:** Leigh Clapp.
5. P: Trevor Fox.
LOOK TO THE TROPICS Pg 148
1. P: Leigh Clapp. **2. P:** Lorna Rose.
3. P: Leigh Clapp. **4. P:** Leigh Clapp.
5. P: Leigh Clapp. **6. P:** Leigh Clapp.
7. P: Leigh Clapp. **8. P:** Leigh Clapp.
Pg 149 P: David Young.
Pg 150 P: Leigh Clapp.
Pg 151 P: Leigh Clapp.

SMALL GARDENS PLANT GUIDE
POTS Pg 152 1. P: Leigh Clapp.
2. P: Leigh Clapp. **3. P:** Leigh Clapp.
4. P: Leigh Clapp. **5. P:** Leigh Clapp.
Pg 153 6. P: Leigh Clapp. **7. P:** Leigh Clapp. **8. P:** Dan Magree. **9. P:** Leigh Clapp.
Pg 154 1. P: Leigh Clapp. **2. P:** Trisha Dixon.
Pg 155 3. P: Trisha Dixon. **4. P:** Trisha Dixon. **5. P:** Trisha Dixon. **6. P:** Leigh Clapp. **7. P:** Leigh Clapp. **8. P:** Trisha Dixon.
TREES Pg 156 1. P: Leigh Clapp.
2. P: Trisha Dixon. **3. P:** Ester Beaton.
4. P: Ivy Hansen. **5. P:** Leigh Clapp.
6. P: Lorna Rose.
Pg 157 7. P: Leigh Clapp.

COAST TO COUNTRY
Pg 158-163 P: Simon Griffiths.
GD: Fiona Brockhoff's Landscape Design, Sorrento, Vic.
Pg 164, 165 P: Leigh Clapp.
Pg 166, 167 P: Leigh Clapp.
Pg 168, 169 P: Ray Joyce. **GD:** Elaine Rushbrooke, The Scented Rose, Glaziers Bay, Tasmania.
Pg 170, 171 P: Nigel Noyes.
Pg 172, 173 P: Nigel Noyes. Sculpture by Folko Kooper.
Pg 174, 175 P: Leigh Clapp.
Pg 178, 179 P: Dan Magree.
Pg 180 P: Dan Magree.
Pg 182, 183 P: Dan Magree.
Pg 184, 185 P: Leigh Clapp.
Pg 186, 187 P: Leigh Clapp.

Editor-in-chief Anny Friis

Art director Hieu Nguyen
Picture editor Alexandra Neuman
Copy editor Lynda Wilton
Horticultural consultant Jennifer Stackhouse
Text Jennifer Stackhouse Rose-Marie Hillier Allison Tait Paul Urquhart

Publishing manager (sales) Brian Cearnes
Publishing manager (rights & new projects) Jane Hazell
Brand manager Donna Gianniotis
Production manager Carol Currie
Business manager Sally Lees
Studio manager Caryl Wiggins
Pre-press Harry Palmer
Editorial coordinator Caroline Lowry
Editorial assistant Karen Lai

Chief executive officer John Alexander
Group publisher Jill Baker
Publisher Sue Wannan
Editorial director Susan Tomnay

Produced by ACP Books
Printed in China by Leefung-Asco Printers
Published by ACP Publishing Pty Limited, 54 Park Street, Sydney, NSW 2000
(GPO Box 4088, Sydney, NSW 2001),
phone (02) 9282 8618, fax (02) 9267 9438, acpbooks@acp.com.au and www.acpbooks.com.au
AUSTRALIA: Distributed by Network Services, GPO Box 4088, Sydney, NSW 2001,
phone (02) 9282 8777, fax (02) 9264 3278
UNITED KINGDOM: Distributed by Australian Consolidated Press (UK), Moulton Park Business Centre,
Red House Road, Moulton Park, Northampton, NN3 6AQ,
phone (01604) 497 531, fax (01604) 497 533, acpukltd@aol.com
CANADA: Distributed by Whitecap Books Ltd, 351 Lynn Avenue, North Vancouver, BC, V7J 2C4,
phone (604) 980 9852
NEW ZEALAND: Distributed by Netlink Distribution Company, ACP Media Centre, Cnr Fanshawe and
Beaumont Streets, Westhaven, Auckland (PO Box 47906, Ponsonby, Auckland, NZ),
phone (9) 366 9966, ask@ndcnz.co.nz

Garden.

Includes index.
ISBN 1 86396 317 0.
1. Gardening – Australia. I. Title: Australian House & Garden.

635.0994

© ACP Publishing Pty Limited 2003
ABN 18 053 273 546
This publication is copyright. No part of it may be reproduced or transmitted in any form without the
written permission of the publishers. First published in 2003.

Front cover: The Scented Rose, Glaziers Bay, Tasmania. Photography by Ray Joyce.